T0129040

IDENTITY

WHO WE WERE | WHO WE ARE | WHO WE SHALL BECOME

JERMAINE M. HARRIS

EDITED BY

BRANDY A. HARRIS

authorHOUSE®

AuthorHouse™
1663 Liberty Drive
Bloomington, IN 47403
www.authorhouse.com
Phone: 1-800-839-8640

First published by AuthorHouse   08/25/2011

ISBN: 978-1-4634-4162-3 (sc)
ISBN: 978-1-4634-4161-6 (ebk)

Library of Congress Control Number: 2011913022

Printed in the United States of America

Any people depicted in stock imagery provided by Thinkstock are models, and such images are being used for illustrative purposes only.
Certain stock imagery © Thinkstock.

This book is printed on acid-free paper.

Table of Contents

The purpose of this workbook

The information contained within this workbook is to enlighten and inspire two groups of African Americans; the first group is the people who are unaware of the cultural history of African Americans. The second group is the people who are aware of the cultural history, yet are compelled to sit with people from the first group and discuss the topics within.

This book was created by Black Family United, a non-profit organization that is committed to creating a common movement of cultural evaluation for the purpose of cultural improvement. Through the theory of "emotion evaluation", we suggest that the core functions of a particular culture can be studied by focusing on that group's use of the 14 basic emotions. Thus this book breaks down what those emotions are, and how African Americans have used those emotions to create their culture. Additionally, this workbook creates room for specific dialogue between student and teacher / child and parent / mentor and mentee to promote understanding and a paradigm shift in how African Americans use those basic emotions.

Our ultimate goal is to give the people the power to influence their own happiness, strengthen their own understanding and improve themselves for generations to come. The way we quantify the success of a culture is by examining the following:

Marriage rate	Divorce rate
Rate of single parent households	Incarceration rate
High school drop out rate	College graduation rate

In studying the trends of these statistics, it is our hope that these numbers will change towards the better due to our research and outreach. The improvement of these numbers will represent African Americans living harmoniously within emotionally healthy relationships. This harmony is good for the African American child, the African American family, the entire U.S. citizenship as well as the world at-large.

Living without evaluation and corrective action in all aspects of life, is likened to driving while blindfolded. Let's join our hearts and minds on one accord and a shared goal with a common solution to avoid a deadly crash. Ask yourself, what can I do to improve; what can I do to help? Give your time, energy and thought to make a change.

Be significant,

Mickey Chavis
Vice Chairman
BlackFamilyUnited.org

Letter to the Student

This book is written for you. You are our future. As your elders, we feel that if you fail, we fail. As African Americans we have been failing lately. This book is to give you some choices to consider regarding your future. Each one of you have a unique set of circumstances, with benefits and obstacles to overcome, as we all do. This book will take you step by step through a thought process so you can better understand life's options and obligations.

In every group of students there are those who are not interested. They may be disengaged and unwilling to open their minds to new ideas. Most people in that situation are dealing with circumstances that appear unfair to them. Most adults understand that fact, but many don't know what to do about it. So you are left to fend for yourself and fight the forces against you. This book is dedicated to those few students who think the world is against them. The authors of this book are on your team. We encourage you to continue to fight the injustice and inequities of your situation. Yet we suggest that you use the same energy slightly different. If you were to use that energy in the way this book prescribes, you will beat the odds. You can win that same fight, just by using different tactics.

World champion boxers often lose their title and get their belt stripped from them. That's where you may be right now. You were born a champion, but you may have been dealt a devastating blow in life. Now it's time to get up, dust yourself off, make this book your training manual and start training for the fight of your life. Learn the boxing game of life, study it and understand it. Practice practice practice, and prepare yourself for battle. With the right mindset and the right information in your corner, you will be VICTORIOUS.

Letter to the Instructor

Thank you for purchasing this workbook. This book was developed by Black Family United, a non-profit organization whose mission is to create and reinforce efforts and options for the continual moral development of the African American community. The core focus of BFU is to encourage the healthiest environments possible to raise emotionally balanced African American children.

The particular way that we are focusing on the African American population is by presenting options in a way that are appealing to the African American culture. The particular reason we focus on the African American population is because of the relatively high negative statistics, and the relatively low positive statistics.

The first step in using this workbook effectively is to review the concepts and find solace in its message. In other words, by instructing from this book, you are not professing to be perfect, yet you must believe in the message and find applicability of this message within your own personal experiences.

Each passage is a potential class discussion topic. We encourage the instructor to review each passage and prepare for probable questions and conversations that may arise. There are several concepts and applications within this book, and we commission you to reshape and adapt the principles and activities to best suit the comprehension level of your particular students. We also encourage you to participate in our on-line forum.

Toward the back of this book is the Group Activities section, which serves as a reinforcement of the principles discussed in the workbook. These activities shall allow you to drive home the concepts with physical movement and role play to enrich the experience and hopefully make a deeper impact on the lives of all who partake.

If you have not already done so, please register at www.africanamericanidentity.org. By becoming a life time member of our community of instructors, you will chat about your personal experiences with each of the group activities and classroom discussions. This will help all instructors in their presentation development. We also encourage you to share group activities that you may create that emphasize the concepts and principles within the book.

Each activity will be rated on a scale from 1 to 5 stars by all instructors on-line according to the activities effectiveness. The activities that are in print that are rated low will be removed from future editions, and the activities created by instructors that receive high ratings will be incorporated in new editions.

Lastly, the back of the book entitled "Intake" serves as a long term approach to student success. This section will give tips and materials on how to become a more impactful person in the lives of the young people you coach. Many youth have people such as yourself, in their lives for a short season, thus this workbook and the on-line tool encourages you to develop a longer term relationship with the students that need more of your encouragement. To enhance your life's good works, we assist you in tracking and monitoring these children's success by being involved for the long haul. This support and love is what the book encourages. We look to you as a doer of this good work. We hope to affectively assist you.

Letter to the Parents

Statistics tend to show African American male students as being laggards in most categories with behavioral problems. School systems, teachers and parents have been at odds for the past 30 years regarding this data. This book really does not contemplate or argue the current state of the three parties just mentioned. Our focus is not regarding reading skills, math scores or writing abilities. We are only focused on student's citizenship. This book covers principles of how each student feels about themselves and how they treat everyone around them. We feel that these are the neglected building block to academic and life's successes.

We are BlackFamilyUnited.org, and we have formed to assist African Americans in transcending their history. We understand that some parents may feel negatively about these concepts, and they may elect to have their children excluded from this workbooks review. If that is the case for you, please discuss that point with the instructor. However, we urge you to revisit the purpose of this book and its potential positive impact on the children that do participate.

With the understanding that it takes a village to raise a child, we also understand that the village must have the same core values. We at Black Family United feel as if many in our population do not share common values for a number of reasons. Yet we extend our resources to ALL that raise our children to make the right choices in life. If your child(ren) do not have such issues, they will most definitely deal with people in this world with such issues. This book addresses how they should interact with all types of people.

> **Your child(ren) may have various questions about life, that may be unsettling for you. This is why we encourage you to take a proactive approach in dealing with these concepts in order to have fruitful interactions with your child(ren).**

We at BlackFamilyUnited.org encourage you to visit us on-line and share with us your opinion and experiences with this book. All constructive feedback is welcome; we'd love to hear from you. www.africanamericanidentity.org.

Live the Change,

Jermaine Harris
Executive Director - Author
BlackFamilyUnited.org

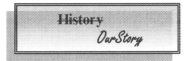

History
Our Story

Slavery was not unique to the Americas, but was known to have existed in civilizations such as ancient Egypt, Assyria, ancient Greece and parts of the Roman Empire. These slave institutions were made up of a mixture of debt-slavery, punishment for crime, the enslavement of prisoners of war, and the birth of children of slaves.

The first Africans arrived in the western hemisphere in 1494 with Christopher Columbus on his second voyage to Hispaniola. These Africans were free persons. This book will concentrate on the Atlantic slave trade which is customarily divided into two eras, known as the First and Second Atlantic Systems.

The First Atlantic System was started around 1500, with slaves being provided by the Portuguese. They had been kidnapping and trading for African slaves since 1444. The Spanish soon joined in, by issuing merchants from other countries the license to trade slaves to their American colonies. By 1502, the African slave trade to the Americas had developed to a significant scale and lasted until around 1580. Although some Dutch, English, Spanish and French traders participated in the first era, the Portuguese were the largest suppliers of slave labor.

The second era was mainly controlled by the British, Portuguese, French and Dutch traders during the 17th, 18th and 19th centuries. The three main destinations of this phase were the Caribbean colonies, Brazil, and North America.

The first slaves used by Europeans in what later became the United States were brought by would-be Spanish colonizers of North Carolina in 1526. The colonization attempt was a failure, lasting only one year; the slaves revolted and fled into the wilderness to live free among the Native Americans.

In 1619, the year that is most commonly identified as the beginning of slavery in the United States, approximately twenty Africans were brought by a Dutch soldier on the *White Lion* ship and sold to Governor Yeardley and other merchants in the English colony of Old Point Comfort. Governor Yeardly purchased seven of the Africans and transported them twenty-five miles to

Jamestown, Virginia, as indentured servants. However, there were a small number of blacks, approximately 32, living in the settlement at the time, and it is not known if they were free or enslaved.

The progression from indentured servitude to racial slavery happened slowly. It was not until the House of Burgesses of Virginia passed the Slave Codes of 1705, removing any uncertainty that the status of Africans and African Americans as slaves would be solidified. The Codes served as a model for the other colonies to follow. The slave status for Africans and their descendants would last for 160 years, until after the end of the Civil War with the ratification of the 13th Amendment in December of 1865.

This chapter highlights the lives of under-appreciated, African American slaves and their descendants. Although the vestiges of slavery have placed a serious burden on the shoulders of the African Americans of today, they must seek the truth of this institution, as well as allow the knowledge of its existence to build resolve to be successful. Many of the African American people within the twentieth century have allowed the knowledge, or lack of knowledge of the slave trade to become a crutch or an excuse not to strive for success and to accept mediocrity in their own lives. This fact has significantly shaped our world view. The lack of truth within our standard educational system leaves ambiguity in the minds of African American students. The goal of this chapter is to give an overview of not only the occurrences, but also the incentive for positive interpretation of the African American experience. We must distinguish that our worst enemy is ignorance; and our best ally is our full participation in this democratic society.

History is not an adults-only game as you will discover. Yet it is the responsibility of the adults to place the truth before our young African Americans in a way that builds pride and determination to continue to lift and improve the African American experience. This may be accomplished by being eager participants in the pursuit of education, developing a strong personal character and economic wealth. Hopefully, you will find inspiration in these following pages.

Inventors & Innovators

By 1913 over 1,000 inventions were patented by African Americans. Among the most notable inventors were:

Elijah McCoy (1843–1929) invented automatic lubrication devices for steam engines. Other inventors tried to copy McCoy's oil-dripping cup. But none of the other cups worked as well as his, so customers started asking for "the real McCoy." That's where the expression comes from.

Lewis Howard Latimer (1848–1928) invented an improvement for the incandescent light bulb. Latimer worked in the laboratories of both Thomas Edison and Alexander Graham Bell.

Jan Matzeliger (1852–1889) developed the first machine to mass-produce shoes. In 1992, the U.S. made a postage stamp in honor of Matzeliger.

Granville Woods (1856–1910) had 35 patents to improve electric railway systems, including the first system to allow moving trains to communicate. Woods left school at age 10 to work and support his family.

Dr. Daniel Hale Williams (1856-1931) the founder of Provident Hospital and performed the first successful open heart surgery.

George Washington Carver (1860–1943) developed peanut butter and 400 plant products. Carver was born a slave. He didn't go to college until he was 30.

Garrett A. Morgan (1877–1963) developed the first automatic traffic signal and gas mask.

Charles Drew (1904-1950) A pioneer in the field of blood preservation, he developed a method for separating plasma from the whole blood so they could be combined later. He also determined that plasma could be administered to certain patients regardless of their blood type and helped to establish the modern blood bank.

Vivien Theodore Thomas (1910-1985) was the first African American without a doctorate degree to perform open heart surgery on a white patient in the United States. He was a surgical technician who developed the procedures used to treat blue baby syndrome in the 1940s. Without any education past high school, Thomas became a cardiac surgery pioneer and teacher of operative techniques to many of the country's most prominent surgeons.

Shirley Anita St. Hill Chisholm (1924-2005) was a Congresswoman, representing New York's 12th Congressional District for seven terms from 1969 to 1983. In 1968, she became the first black woman elected to Congress. On January 25, 1972, she became the first major-party black candidate for President of the United States and the first woman to run for the Democratic presidential nomination

Dr. Mark Dean (1957-) received a Ph.D. in Electrical Engineering from Stanford in 1992. He holds three of the original nine patents on the computer.

Dr. Mae C. Jemison (1956-) a pioneering astronaut who entered Stanford University at the age of 16, receiving a B.S. in chemical engineering and a B.A. in African and Afro-American Studies. Jemison obtained her doctorate of Medicine degree from Cornell Medical College. Jemison joined the staff of the Peace Corps and served as a Peace Corps Medical Officer from 1983 to 1985 responsible for the health of Peace Corps Volunteers serving in Liberia and Sierra Leone. In 1987 she was accepted into the NASA astronaut program and  in 1992 flew on the shuttle endeavor into outer space. Jemison logged 190 hours, 30 minutes, 23 seconds in space.

These inventors and innovators make their mark on the world in spite of the great odds against them. They overcame the inequalities that existed within the society. Education is the study of who created and discovered what in the past. With that knowledge you can contribute to your chosen field of study. What invention or contribution will you share with the world?

Selfhood

> *"Change will not come if we wait for some other person or some other time. We are the ones we've been waiting for. We are the change that we seek"*
> **Barack Obama**

> *"A winner is a winner even before he wins"*
> **Berry Gordy**

Selfhood defined

Self is a person. The suffix "hood" is the state of being. Selfhood is a person's knowledge of ones self. As a person becomes increasingly conscious of their personality and identity he/she grows a stronger sense of selfhood.

Mastery of Selfhood is a goal common to those who want to obtain wisdom and enlightenment. This is the process of understanding why you do what you do and what effect your actions have on the world. This will enable you to gain a higher level of inner-strength to change your actions and priorities in order to become a better person.

A good way to strive for mastery of Selfhood is to consciously work on developing a strong personal Philosophy of Life (POL). This POL should use various principles of life to represent a path that leads to a distinct identity or individuality that brings peace, joy and harmony to the world.

Selfhood Synonyms

character, circumstances, coherence,

distinctiveness, existence, identification, individualism,

individuality, integrity, oneness, particularity, personality,

self, selfdom, selfness, singleness, singularity, status,

uniqueness

Topic for discussion

How should a person develop his/her own philosophy of life?

Man Know Thyself

In many ancient African cultures as well as many ancient Asian cultures there have been long periods of inner focus. This focus was based on understanding an individuals place within nature as an integral part of nature. Western European culture for most of history has not been focused on individuals place within nature, but the individual's dominance over nature. These stark differences in philosophies both have their advantages and disadvantages.

Ancient Africans slowly began to shift from a pure form of oneness with nature, to a dominance of nature. During this time they also began to lose power of inner peace and tranquility with the Earth. They began to place value of material wealth and political power over the importance of being at peace with man and nature. As Africans began to have greater contact with Europeans, they begin to adapt the values of those Europeans they traded with. African tribes began to war on a much more frequent and increasingly violent level. The culture of oneness with nature and respect for man was diminishing. This new culture and thirst lead to Africans participation in the African slave trade with the Portuguese traders.

Topic for discussion
Did you know that Africans participated in the slave trade? How does this fact change your thoughts about slavery?

Throughout the Africans dealing with the Europeans, Africans increased deadly wars against their rival tribes. Though the method of divide and conquer was a regular tactic of European traders, the contribution to the slave trade that Africans made should be an awakening fact for African Americans. As Africans increased inter-tribal warfare over scarce resources and valuable trade artifacts, they found that enemies could be captured and used as trading ponds with the Europeans. This major contribution to the slave trade by Africans should deny the reasoning of blaming Europeans solely for the slave trade. Many African Americans have developed a reluctance to interact with European descendants due to the fact that Europeans enslaved Africans. Yet to place full blame on a partial participant is not as effective or productive as understanding all who contributed; therefore forgiving the past so one can move into the future with confidence is crucial for our growth as a people.

Topic for discussion
Discuss why anger over slavery can make future success difficult.

Ma'at

The word Ma'at (pronounced- My-at) originated in ancient Egypt. In its simplest definition, it means a continual expression of love. Yet to fully encompass the meaning of Ma'at, it takes much more than a simple sentence. Ma'at is balance, truth, justice, peace, fellowship and righteousness. It is a lifestyle that an individual can chose to live. This lifestyle displays wisdom through correct judgment of choices in life. The most similar western concept to Ma'at is living a "Christ-like" life. This lifestyle is very difficult to fully obtain, but is an admirable goal. Ancient Africans believed that Ma'at can be bestowed upon a person as they draw closer to their God, as God grants them "divine wisdom."

One of the primary principals to embrace while attempting to live a life of Ma'at is to strictly adhere to the law of sympathy. The law of sympathy states that two like things are attracted to one another. So in attempting to change your life, you must simply desire and admire those things, people and symbols of that lifestyle. In doing so, you will be attracted to that lifestyle and eventually adopt the qualities of that lifestyle.

PURSUING MA'AT

1. Seek through appreciation

2. Wisdom

3. Law of Causation

4. Love

In changing your life towards a path of Ma'at, you can first start with seeking and appreciating all things that display balance, truth, justice, peace, fellowship and righteousness. If you want to be an honest person, associate with honest people. If you want to be a smart person, do what smart people do. If you want to be righteous, study the meaning and the historical use of the word righteous. Once you build many experiences, you will find your personality changing to mimic and become the person you desire to be. But you must realize that this means that you have to disassociate yourself from things that work against your chosen path. To disassociate yourself from elements that you do not like does not mean to continue to dislike them. You must grow indifferent to them, so that you don't even notice them any longer. This will take the power of influence away and you will stop being effected by those things that you do not wish to encounter.

> **Topic for discussion**
>
> Discuss the different ways that a person can practice Ma'at

Every person has personality traits and unique characteristics. Each person is born with a basic personality skeleton, but it is further shaped and developed by ones environment and experiences. Hence you can control your personality by controlling your environment or embracing the good aspects of your environment and rejecting the negative aspects of your environment. What makes this concept of control difficult is immaturity or a lack of wisdom to know how today's events will affect tomorrow's reality.

So the second point to focus on is wisdom. If you seek wisdom, it will seek you. The opposite is true as well, if you accept ignorance, it will surely stay with you. To seek wisdom, you must open your eyes and mind to the "law of cause and effect" which states: Every action has a reaction. The law of cause and effect states that all physical, or spiritual energy [or metaphysical] occurrences are a result of a prior energy. Wisdom is the understanding: "if I do this, then that is most likely to happen." Or, "if I avoid doing this, then that will be less likely to happen." So by rationally thinking, you can have more control over your future compared to if you never tried to understand the law of cause and effect. Without rational thinking, you are more affected by the environment as opposed to you effecting your environment.

> *"Who or WHAT is your leader? You can't change your direction, unless you change your leader."*
> **Pastor Eddie Seals**

The third point to focus on is referred to as the Law of Causation, also known as karma or "you will reap, what you sow" *[If you sow (plant) a bad seed, you may live off of bad fruit that you reap (harvest) and never know how sweet your fruit could have been if you sown (planted) good seeds].*

> **Example:**
> Person #1 hurt person #2
> Person #2 who then gets mad, hurts person #3
> Person #3 in turn hurts person #4
> Person #4 eventually because of being hurt by person #3 ends up hurting person #5.
> Karma is when person #5 is person #1's son, mother, brother or best-friend?

This law states that the nature or type of energy that you put into the universe will eventually return to you. This concept is important to understand in Ma'at because it becomes a driving force in how you treat other people. If you lack the ability to sympathize or care for others, but you understand that being mean to others may eventually cause you personal harm, you may be influenced to treat others with respect and dignity. This universal law is so broad that Karma may not return to you in the same form that you put it into the world, but if what you put into the universe is negative, you will attract negative energy back to you. You often times will never know that negative karma has come back to you. You may simply miss a great opportunity in life and not know it was ever an opportunity.

For example: If you were mean to Terry a year ago, and Terry told James about "your character" in a negative way, James may have a job opening that he would have offered to you, but he decides not to because of what Terry has told him about your character or

Topic for discussion

Discuss the belief or disbelief in karma

judgment. You may not have even liked the job, but if you would have received the job, you may have met particular people who would present grand opportunities for future success and happiness. Yet, due to something you did last year, it causes you to miss out on realizing your dreams or enjoying a fulfilling life experience.

Lastly, is the concept of love. The three points of love are to love yourself, love others and love every living thing. When you do things to express your love, that is Ma'at. Loving yourself is something that most people think they do automatically. But in actuality, many of us do not love ourselves properly. Think of all the things you would change about yourself if you had the opportunity. Think of all the things that you've done to put yourself in harms way and taken an unnecessary risk. You should attempt to love yourself regardless of what "flaws" you may think you have.

Loving others is the most difficult task. Many of us think that we should not or would not love anyone that does not either love us or deserve our love. Ma'at teaches us that we must learn to love those people regardless of what they do or deserve. By practicing

Topic for discussion

Do you think it is possible or difficult to love someone that hurt you?

this aspect of Ma'at, we are practicing Godly love, which is love that is unconditional. Loving others is simply wanting the best outcome for people. Even regarding people who may have hurt you in the past, you must honestly want the best for them. The best may be for them to understand their bad ways and find the desire to change. If you wish for them to change so that they no longer hurt people in the future, you are wishing that love spreads throughout the world. If you wish for bad things to happen to them, instead of wishing the best for a person that has hurt you, you just create more negative energy. These individuals may not learn a lesson, and may continue to hurt people.

"Hurt people tend to hurt people"

If someone hurts you, and you wish bad things to happen to that person, you are more likely to hurt someone else. So to avoid this, you must learn to forgive people that may have hurt you in the past. This will free you from hurting others and allow you to seek more happiness.

> **Topic for discussion**
>
> "Hurt people tend to hurt people"
> What do you think that means?

The opposite of Ma'at is "isfet", which means untruth, falsehood, disorder and disharmony. You should avoid living life in this state of mind. This is considered an <u>abomination of God</u>. In other words, it is very displeasing to God or the natural order of people seeking peace and happiness. By creating <u>Chaos</u>, you may find a temporary sense of excitement and happiness, but in the long run it leads to destruction. Wickedness may gain wealth, power and prestige, but Ma'at wins over time.

Activity: Judging others

THE FOURTEEN BASIC EMOTIONS

There are fourteen basic emotions within each human being. Seven are feel-good emotions, and seven are feel-bad emotions. Emotions are biochemical reactions within our bodies that change our moods. The average healthy baby is born with the ability to feel all fourteen emotions. As we grow up, we learn from other people through experience, how to use, express or hold back our emotions. Often times we learn how to use our emotions inappropriately. As we grow closer to adulthood, we should try to understand how we use our emotions. With this knowledge, we can begin to change how we use our emotions more effectively. Your use of emotions is what makes you succeed or fail in life. If you improperly use your emotions by relying on the negative emotions too much, you may not accomplish many goals in life. But if you learn to depend on feel-good emotions more than the negative ones, you will be in a better position to accomplish your ultimate goal.

Emotional response is the differentiating factor between cultures. Even though all people are born with these same 14 basic emotions, we use and express our emotions according to our cultural norms. These norms may tell boys not to cry, not to show weakness, not to learn to feel and express particular emotions. These norms, rules or expectations may be to the benefit of the culture, or these rules may be a hindrance. Once these rules create a negative situation for the culture as a whole, then that group must look at how they teach their young to process and express their emotions in order to improve the status and benefits to the people of that culture.

The cultural norms, or emotional responses must align with the ultimate goals of the individuals. If you don't know what your ultimate goal is, then allow this book to tell you what it should be:

"INNER-PEACE THROUGH HAPPINESS"

You may think your ultimate goal is to become an entertainer, a doctor or a parent. These things may be great goals, but your ultimate goal should always be to obtain peace through happiness. What does that phrase mean to you? Ask yourself, does becoming a doctor guarantee your happiness. Does becoming a world famous entertainer guarantee your peace of mind? The answer is unmistakably NO.

FEEL-GOOD EMOTIONS	FEEL-BAD EMOTIONS
Enthusiasm	Fear
Passion	Hate
Desire	Guilt
Hope	Grief
Faith	Anger
Love	Jealousy
Lust	Loneliness

See if you can think of any other emotions that are not synonyms with any of the terms listed. Some words may be a combination of a few different emotions, such as compassion/sympathy/empathy, which are all different mixtures of love, fear and guilt.

Topic for discussion
Discuss emotional situations you have been in and how you reacted inappropriately?

12

Some words may be similar, but a different degree of one of the above words. For example, excessive anger may cause rage. Rage is anger that causes a person to lose control of their selves. Even though we have little control over our emotions, rage is an example where your emotions can control you. Many people in prison find themselves in prison because they allowed their anger to get out of control. Some words you may think of may not be emotions, but reactions to emotions. Revenge is an example that is not an emotions, it is a response to anger, hate, fear or jealousy.

Not all feel-good emotions are positive to a particular person at a particular time. As well, not all feel-bad emotions are negative to a particular person at a particular time. Some feel –good emotions cause more problems in a persons life if unchecked, additionally, without some feel-bad emotions, a person may suffer more problems.

> **Topic for discussion**
>
> What feel-good emotions are bad, and what feel-bad emotions are good? Discuss the circumstances.

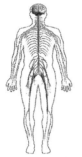

Depression and anxiety are very prominent problems within the African American community that normally go unaddressed. These feelings are a result of an overall emotional imbalance when a person is experiencing too many feel-bad emotions and not enough feel-good emotions. If left untreated, it will lead to health issues such as high blood pressure, hyper tension and certain cancers and heart problems. These diseases are more common in the African American community relative to the society at large; and ultimately lead to a shorter life span and lower quality of life. Our culture plays a role in determining how we use our emotions; our emotions determine our stress level; our stress level determines our health; our health determines how long we live.

Emotions are created within the brain based on ones environment. The brain creates a unique mixture of chemicals and sends them through the blood stream and nervous system. If the brain produces too many feel-bad emotions with not enough feel-good emotions to act as a balance, the body may respond with shock, depression or anxiety.

Shock is caused by a sudden traumatic event that causes your nervous system to instantly malfunction; it is normally dominated by fear. Depression is when your nervous system shuts down slowly and is very slow to recover; it is normally dominated by guilt (or shame which is a subsection of guilt). Anxiety is the over-reaction of your nervous system that causes confusion; it can be dominated by a combination of more than one feel-bad emotion. Yet there tends to be an extreme lack of the positive emotions hope and faith.

The African American culture normally relates faith to religion. Yet these words are not the same. People who do not believe in religion or divine existence, may still posses faith. Faith is having the feeling that everything will work out for the better in the future. Religious people believe that God's plan protects their future. Therefore they have faith in his protection. Hope on the other hand, tends to have more uncertainty regarding future outcomes. Without either hope or faith, a person will tend not to plan for the future, which may limit their potential for growth.

Another response a person can have is no emotion at all. This is called indifference or apathy. This response can be very helpful in trying to get rid of a feel-bad emotion. For example, if someone talks negatively about your mother, it may be so enraging that you want to get revenge and attack that person. If you attempt to replace the emotional response of rage, with the non-emotional response of indifference, you are actively removing that person's power and control to ruin your day. This can bring you closer to inner-peace and happiness.

Activity: Words that bind

A negative example of using indifference is to replace a positive emotion with indifference. So instead of acting as if you love or feel guilt, you act as if you don't care. So if someone was walking in front of you and they accidently fell and hurt themselves, you won't respond with compassion and concern and help them, but your may step right over them and not ask them if they are okay.

> **Topic for discussion**
>
> Discuss personal examples of using indifference?

An example of using indifference in a positive way is to learn to change your normal response of the negative emotions of lust, with indifference. Lust is often times distracting and reduces people focus on other things that may be very important. So in order to be able to study and focus better, a person can replace lust with indifference. Desensitization is when you do not feel emotion that the average person would feel in a particular situation. This is usually socially unhealthy. It takes you away from Ma'at because without the ability to have emotions regulate how you feel, you become more capable of doing things that cause others harm, or you may be less willing to assist people in need.

14

Desensitization most commonly happens when someone is exposed to a situation too early in life, or too frequently. For example, if a 7 year old child is exposed to R rated movies, he/she may not be able to understand or properly process what they are being exposed to. This creates an inappropriate understanding of the content of the movie.

An example of overexposure that causes desensitizing is a soldier in combat. If he sees a lot of death and destruction, he may be desensitized by death and not associate a feel-bad emotion to death. He could become a killing machine that can kill with no regard for human life. In today's society our children are being overexposed to many things through the media and other sources. If parents do not adequately guard their children from overexposure or premature exposure, it will have a negative effect on the emotional development of that child.

I don't want what's best for me

Cognitive dissonance (discomfort) is a brain function that makes a person choose wrong over right, even though they know better. When a person thinks that they cannot afford the

> **Topic for discussion**
>
> Is ignorance really bliss?

right choice, or they feel as if the right choice is not a possible option, they justify or glorify the wrong choice. They change their attitude, beliefs and actions so that the wrong choice is something that they can live with. They ignore the bad effects of their decision as they feel they do not have a choice. When an entire group, community or sub-culture embraces harmful customs due to cognitive dissonance, they tend to suffer the negative consequences in the long run.

Maslow's Hierarchy of Needs

Abraham Maslow wrote a paper in 1943 entitled *A Theory of Human Motivation*. He determined that in order to be motivated to do big things, you must first obtain a basic level of happiness. So motivation is built upon happiness. To summarize this theory:

- *If you are always hungry or suffer from mal-nutrition, you will only be motivated to find food to eat, and other functions will not be successful.*
- *If you don't feel safe and protected from danger, you will only focus on safety, and other functions will not be successful.*
- *If you lack love and belonging from a group, you will be focused on being accepted in a group, and other functions will not be successful.*

Living on an overdose of Adrenaline

Adrenaline is a chemical that your body produces in stressful situations. This chemical creates a physical readiness to respond to danger or hostile environments. It creates a "Fight or Flight" response in you that allows you to protect yourself. Slavery created a need for the slaves to overproduce adrenaline in order to survive immediate danger. Two hundred and fifty years later, there are segments of the African American culture that are still overproducing adrenaline. They are overdosing on adrenaline. Adrenaline makes the mind only focus on the immediate future. Yet when a high dose of adrenaline is present within the body, it is difficult to think long-term and focus on the long-term effects of ones current actions.

By overdosing on adrenaline, people tend to do things for immediate gratification and neglect the long-term effects of their immediate gratification. They feel that they will enjoy today and worry about the future tomorrow. But when tomorrow comes, they have to worry due to the lack of planning yesterday. This creates more adrenaline. With the adrenaline, they are making a decision not based on what may turn out the best tomorrow. This is a vicious cycle that is taught from generation to generation. This way of living and processing emotions with an overdose of adrenaline is called the "slave mentality."

> **Topic for discussion**
>
> Can you think of examples of the slave mentality and its harmful affects?

Love vs. Hate

Love is a feel-good emotion that is required to become an emotionally healthy person. There are many levels, types and depths of love, yet to see the most simple and broadest view of love we can compare love to other optional emotions a person can have. You can view everything and everyone in one of three ways:

| Hate | Indifference | Love |

Hate is a feel-bad emotion that affects the hater more than the person that they hate. Love is a feel-good emotion that affects the lover as well as the loved. Indifference is the lack of an emotion, therefore there is no positive or negative exchange of emotional energy. The power of Ma'at comes from creating more and more positive emotional energy. To "effectively" love someone is to wish the best for them, and to not knowingly do anything to hurt them.

Dysfunctional Families

You can have people in your life that love you, and wish the best for you, but they knowingly or unknowingly hurt you or disregard your feelings. You may want to question if they truly love you. In many situations, people do not fully understand why they do things to hurt the people they love. Yet this is an example of "ineffective love." "Dysfunctional families" operate in this way. In situations that arise, people have emotional responses which can be expressed in many different ways. During conflict, dysfunctional people tend to want to share their negative emotions rather than resolve, minimize or avoid conflict. They respond in revengeful ways or disregard other people's feelings.

Many American families are 'Dysfunctional." They tend to unknowingly teach their dysfunction to their younger generations and it creates a pattern. This book is focused on giving you the skills and understanding to break

> **Topic for discussion**
>
> Discuss dysfunction in your family that you'd like to change.

negative cycles of dysfunction within your family. African American culture has internalized many ineffective patterns that may have begun during slavery. African Americans are now free, free to choose how to love and respect one another. You are free to love effectively or ineffectively, it is up to you. Thinking back on your actions, do you honestly treat the people that you love, as if you love them? If you justify treating them badly, they may justify treating you badly. Hence the cycle continues. Someone has to be mature enough to step up and improve the relationship. It is not the burden of the male, the parent, or the oldest sibling, love can change the world regardless of who gives it.

Peace through happiness is achieved by focusing on the 14 emotions. As you mature and grow you should try to understand which emotions you have been taught to use, and which you have been taught not to use. Then think about what people and situations cause you to react in positive and negative ways. Once you start thinking like this and evaluating yourself, you are beginning to seek the wisdom needed to obtain Ma'at. At this point you can try to change how you react emotionally to different situations.

You have a choice to express your emotions whenever you feel them. Or you can stop and think about which emotions are the most appropriate to have and express in order to get the final outcome that you want from a particular situation. The first and quickest responses often times make your situation worse and get you in trouble.

Greed vs. Guilt

As stated above, guilt is a feel-bad emotion. Yet it must be pointed out that even though guilt is a feel-bad emotion, it should not be avoided. Each person should attempt to have the ability to feel a sense of guilt. This is the feeling that helps you to learn to practice right vs. wrong. Many of us in today's society do not have guilt. The lack of guilt is what made it easy to enslave a people with no regard for their right to freedom. During boot camp or army training, guilt is removed from soldiers so he can kill at will. Inner-city gangsters have little guilt while killing someone from a rival gang. Drug dealers feel no guilt while selling poison to people of their own community.

Oftentimes guilt is replaced with greed. Greed is the disregard of other people's feelings, needs and safety in order to obtain personal gain. This greed comes at a great expense to other people. If you were to understand the concept of Greed vs. Guilt and observe how people treat others for the sake of benefiting themselves, you will be on your way to wisdom. If you allow yourself to feel guilt and not ignore that feeling, and not allow greed and selfishness to rule you, you will be on a path towards Ma'at.

Topic for discussion
Is guilt good?

I was taught right but all I see is wrong

It is a great thing to have positive role models in young people's lives so they will be able to witness how to become a positive productive person. Yet, so many people are in a different situation, where they may know right from wrong, but they do not have actual examples of people treating each other with respect and love (living in ma'at). It becomes more of a challenge to break the cycle of a negative environment and become successful in spite of the odds against you. No matter the obstacles, the choice to succeed and the choice to fail is still an individual choice that each person can make on their own. In striving to obtain a happy and successful life is often challenging for everyone. Don't let anyone and any situation convince you that you cannot accomplish great things. Ma'at is available to everyone who simply decides to have it. Remain focused on your hopes and dreams and do not allow others to determine your limits. Do not accept failure and never give up.

CHAPTER NOTES

Thoughts, questions and solutions:

_____
_____
_____
_____
_____
_____
_____

Personal challenges covered in the chapter:

_____
_____
_____

Potential ways to create change in my life/house/community:

_____
_____
_____
_____
_____
_____
_____

Action plan and accountability follow up dates:

_____ _____
_____ _____
_____ _____
_____ _____
_____ _____
_____ _____
_____ _____
_____ _____

Manhood

> *"It is easier to build strong children than to repair broken men"*
>
> **Frederick Douglass**

> *"This ain't fun. But you watch me, I'll get it done."*
>
> **Jackie Robinson**

> *"Swallow your pride and lose the battle to win the war. She's probably right anyway"*
>
> **Jay 'O Speaks**

Man is defined as an adult male human. The suffix "hood" is the state of being. This is very obvious. Yet for the sake of this book, we will delve deeper into the meaning of manhood. We will discuss what a male human has the ability, the option, and the obligation to do. Following that, we will discuss the ramifications and repercussions of many of those decisions.

Activity: Statue of man

Given the various ways manhood could be interpreted, let's create a single definition of manhood within this chapter. Then we can compare this books definition to the types of manhood that has existed throughout African [American] history.

> The definition of Manhood: A male who is <u>willing and able</u> to do at least three of the following four functions for his family:
> PROCREATE, EDUCATE, PROTECT AND PROVIDE

PROCREATE: To conceive a child through sexual intercourse with the opposite sex

EDUCATE: To communicate information that will be used for understanding and future benefit

PROTECT: To keep safe from harm by proactively creating space and barriers between the protected and elements that can cause harm

PROVIDE: To give tangible and intangible substance that is required for survival

The law of Manhood: The law of 3 out of 4 elements must be maintained. However this is only valid if the adults in the family agree on this law. Before going in depth into manhood, let's review other alternatives for males other than manhood.

Malehood: The state of being a male. In contrast to the requirements of manhood, malehood is simply accomplished by being born a male. An adult male is a man, but does not automatically encompass manhood. For the purposes of this text, manhood requires action.

Activity: Hole punch relationships

| EGO |

Throughout history this Latin word Ego meant "I" or the "self" that includes not only the body, but the emotions of a person. The Ego of a person is changed every time there is a change in the person's emotions, or feelings about himself. In modern day times, ego has been equated with ones pride. Hence the term, "bruised ego" which is referring to when some ones pride or confidence is hurt. Regarding men, the American culture has also confused the term "male ego" with the term "manhood." This is a huge mistake, and a correction that we need to make in the African American community.

"I didn't know, I didn't know"
An unknown Black man

The Male ego differs from female ego because the ego depends on emotions. Emotions are caused by different bio-chemical reactions within the brain. Since men have more of a biochemical called testosterone and women have more of a biochemical called estrogen, there is a difference between male and female ego. For the purposes of this chapter, we are only focusing on the ego of the male.

Emotional responses to the environment are often times a learned behavior. These lessons learned are different according to cultural differences. So in reviewing the African American response we can generalize and figure out why different statistics in the African American community exist. Culture tells a male what being a man consist of.

> **Question for discussion**
>
> What are some of the statistics surrounding the African American family?

The difference between manhood and ego is that manhood is not an emotion; it is an action of the four functions mentioned above. Many African American males try to protect their ego, and not pay attention to their manhood. This causes many problems for the man as well as his family. If a man fails at manhood, he will sometimes forget about manhood and just try to protect his ego as he substitutes manhood with ego. Every man's Manhood is tested at some point in his life. When something goes wrong and his manhood is challenged, he can often times feel a negative emotion. He will be faced with the option of continuing to try to improve his manhood with actions that represent manhood, or he can focus on his emotions and respond emotionally. The way

> **Question for discussion**
>
> What does the term "placing the family at risk of danger"

he responds will show if his priority is his manhood or his ego.

The difference in the response of manhood and a response of ego in protecting the family: Response of manhood is when a man responds to a family crisis that results in protecting his family. A response of ego is when a man responds to a family crisis that results in placing his family at risk of danger.

If his response places his family in danger, that is ego. If his response protects his family, that is manhood.

HOOd

When the word "hood" is used in conjunction with the words man, woman or child, it represents the role (expected actions) within the context of a family. For example, if a man is not acting like a protector and provider, his manhood may be at question. Another

Question for discussion

Can a boy have malehood?
Can a boy have manhood?
Can a boy have ego?
Can a man be a man, but have no manhood?
If a man cries, does that affect his manhood?

example is if a child is sexually abused, one may say that that child's childhood has been stolen, because they are now faced with acts that are not of a child. And they may now have to think about and deal with things that are characterized with adulthood.

African American males have unique issues compared to any other male group in America. So we shall cover ancient African males, slave males and current day males. The fearless hunters of Africa that understood the balance of nature were effective for thousands of years within tribal society. Many tribes divided their women according to power and wealth. So a man with multiple wives was common among many African traditions. The male who was able to unite with multiple women had to prove to his potential wife's male tribal elders that he was wise enough, cultured enough and wealthy enough to care for the woman. If he did not meet their standards, he was not granted the woman's hand in marriage. So there was an expectation and a cost to bear in order to qualify as a suitor.

During slavery the African male was stripped of his title of man, thus manhood was impossible in the eyes of the white capturer. The white capturer replaced the manhood of the African and gave him another title that was mutually exclusive to manhood, nigger. This means that a male could not be a man and a nigger at the same time.

Nigger/Nigga This word derives from the first Mid-Atlantic slave traders, the Portuguese. The word "negro" means the color "black", a descendant word of the Latin adjective niger. The word nigger was quickly adapted by Europeans as a derogatory description of African slaves. Given the laws and lack of freedom, Africans were less than human, and closer related to property and animals.

After the slaves were freed in 1865, and before the civil rights victories of 1965, there were two periods, Reconstruction, and the Jim Crow era. Throughout these 100 years, Africans legally turned from being sub-human niggers to being fully free men and women. It was a long and hard battle for freedom that should be a birth right of all American citizens.

Even today, we struggle with our freedom. Parts of the African American community now suffer from mental slavery. They have not let go of a slave mentality, and they continue to embrace those things that take their power away instead of building their power to become men who are filled with manhood. The word nigger/nigga is still used today. Racist white people use it in a derogatory way, rarely in the presence of African Americans; some African Americans use it as a term of endearment and as a negative slur to insult other African Americans.

Many African Americans that use the word argue that the word has a different meaning than it did during the past 400 years. This is a false myth, and the word still has the negative power over those who use it. For example, which of the four African Americans below is more likely to be called nigga by you or anyone else:

An African American prisoner   *An African American President of the United States*
An African American gangster   *An African American Vice President of a large corporation*

It is true that people of the lower part of the socioeconomic latter are more likely to use and accept the use of the word. In fact, most people who use the word would admit to refraining from using it in certain situations where respect and dignity are an expectation, such as church or a job interview. This fact proves that either:

- Using the word lowers your standards of who you are, or

- Those with low standards of who they are use the word.

Either way, the word still carries the negative implications that slave masters intended by calling some one less than human. The same can be said about woman being referred to as a bitch (a female dog is less than human).

If you want to be a man who is strong in manhood and pursues Ma'at, it is suggested that you refrain from using this word and giving it power over the people of your community.

Patriarch A society can either be patriarchal or matriarchal.

> **Patriarchal society** is one in which the male has the dominant authority over institutions, women, children, and property. It implies that females are subordinate or submissive to males.

> **Matriarchal society** is one in which females, especially mothers, have the dominant roles of political leadership and moral authority. This type of society has been rare throughout history, yet has been found to exist in remote cultures throughout the Africa and Asian continents. It is unclear if any African Americans are descendents of such societies, but African Americans of today are faced with a unique family dynamic due to the nature of the African slave trade.

Manhood is different in patriarchal societies than in matriarchal societies. Patriarchal societies require much more inner strength of character. The United States currently is a patriarchal society. Yet the African American sub-culture within the United States is matriarchal. In African tribal cultures there were many different family and social structures. As a stolen people, African Americans do not have information about which tribal cultures they are direct decedents of. However, it is factual that the vast majority of African cultures were patriarchal.

The toll that slavery took on these Africans placed more power and control with the African women, as it took power from the African man. This was an intentional design of slavery. In order to reduce the amount of slave revolts, slave masters designed tactics to break the strength of the male spirit. This made it necessary for the female to become strong to replace the lost in strength of the male. The slave mother is the first teacher of the slave child. To that end, the women were encouraged to raise their sons to be strong in body but weak in mind.

Just as there is a judicial system that includes, capture, prosecution, and incarceration; slavery was structured in the same way. The institution of slavery intentionally reversed the African American dynamic, from a patriarchal society to a matriarchal society. A question that the African Americans culture faces today is:

Is a matriarchal culture acceptable for our future?

Are African American families comfortable with educating their daughters to be the dominant authority of their household (Independent) once the child grows into womanhood? Are African American families intentionally raising sons to be unequipped or unwilling to take the dominant authority role in their future family? Or are these things happening due to external pressures that make the traditional roles relatively difficult to accomplish. We shall review one such external pressure, institutional racism.

Institutional Racism — Institutional racism is the denial of rights or civic benefits of a certain racial or religious group. In the United States institutional racism against African Americans was caused by the dominant population's belief in the inferiority of African Americans. Slowly over recent history this ideology of inferiority has been changing. Less and less people of the dominant race feel as if minorities are inferior. Yet institutional racism continues because of the reality of "Scarce resources." This means that there is a limited amount of openings in private schools and colleges. There are also a limited amount of jobs and money in the economy. Given this scarcity, it is to the advantage of the dominant race to keep resources within their own group in order to maintain their prosperity and current way of life.

Institutional racism is a direct attack on a man's ability to provide for his family. Without the ability to provide material comforts for his family, a man's ego (emotions) will be negatively affected. So a man will have a higher risk of overusing the feel-bad emotions discussed in chapter two. His manhood could be questioned if he and his family do not understand and agree on the Manhood "law of 3 out of 4."

Historically, the African American mans ability to provide for his family has been slowly improving. During slavery the male had little means to provide material wealth. After slavery ended, most of the freed slaves worked on plantations as sharecroppers or farmers. African Americans were concentrated in the South. During the two Great African American Migrations from the South to the North, many African Americans men moved their families north to pursue a better ability to be the Provider. The first Great Migration took place in 1916 to 1929. The Second Great Migration took place from 1941 to 1970. Many landed in Detroit, Chicago and New York in the first migration. California was heavily populated during the second migration. African Americans sought less discrimination, but institutional racism reaches across State lines. There is a large aspect of being a man that provides for a family that institutional racism can not directly effect. Let us take a look at the many ways a man can provide for his family.

| HEY KOOL-AID! |

Kool-aid was a popular soft drink in the African American community for the majority of the 1960's, 1970's and 1980's. It comes in packets that need to be added to water and sugar. Being the provider of Kool-aid in a household is the male role. From a man's perspective he can visualize sitting at the head of the table with his family

sitting around the table with plastic cups stretched out towards him. It is this mans job to continue to fill each family member's cup with the type of Kool-aid that they like. Mommy may like hers unsweetened. Daughter may like hers very sweet. Son may sip his Kool-aid and the baby may drink hers very quickly. Daddy must be quick at pouring Kool-aid.

There are a number of issues that the man has to focus on. Not only are the family members drinking the cups of Kool-aid, but there also may be leaks in some of their cups. Leaks are caused by personality issues that family member's may have. They could have been born with them, or something in their past may have caused a leak. As a leader of the family you have the task of filling all the cups with the right taste of Kool-aid as well as attempting to repair leaks. This is a very difficult task. One may ask:

"How does a man provide an endless supply of Kool-aid?"

Provide: The first step in building an endless supply of Kool-aid, is to first understand each family members needs, or the flavor of Kool-aid they desire. There are obvious material needs such as food, clothing, shelter and heat that a man should work with his adult companion to provide for the entire family. Aside from material needs, and equally as important, a man should also be able and willing to provide the basic needs of emotional support that creates a feeling of emotional security. This security is required for normal and healthy relationship development among all family members.

So if you are the Kool-Aid man for your family, all of the above is how you provide an endless supply of Kool-aid. If you create a Philosophy of Life that is rich in Ma'at, you will be successful in being a Provider.

Protect: To keep safe from harm by proactively creating space and barriers between the family and the elements that can increase the amount of holes in your family members cup. You may protect your family from physical harm by

> **Topics for Discussion:**
>
> What is the difference between imminent danger and potential danger?

making sure no one hurts them physically. But there is much more to protecting a family than fighting for them physically as a response to danger. If someone is threatening your family physically, and you decide to get physical with that person, you may end up in jail for years. Additionally, resorting to violence is not educating your family on how to effectively respond to life's challenges. Who will be there to protect your family while you are in jail? So you have to think of the best ways to accomplish your ultimate goal. You will be called upon to make decisions for the family before they are placed in danger. As the protector of the family you should be aware of the dangers involved with each choice the family makes. For example, if your family wanted to go on vacation to a foreign country, you may have to consider how safe it will be in each country. If your family were to shop for a new car, you may want to consider the safety reports of each choice before buying, to know how well the car withstands car accidents. Protecting is making sure the windows and doors are locked at night. Or walking on the outside of your family while walking down the street, just in case a car pops up on the curb, you will be in a better position to protect your family from harm.

Educate: To communicate information that will help your family avoid getting holes punched in their cup. In order to educate, you must first learn. If you fail to learn about life, then you will not be a good educator. By simply living life, things happen and you have to respond. You should also try to learn as many lessons from difficult situations and mistakes as possible. We all make mistakes at times, but to not learn from your mistakes is true failure. Without learning a lesson, you are bound to make the same mistake again. As well, you will not be able to give good advice or direction to patch up holes that your family members may have. So do not shy away from knowledge, try to absorb different types of knowledge from many different sources so you can be a great educator for your family. From book smart, to street smart and everything in-between, your family needs to be able to rely on you to have good judgment and make the right decisions most of the time.

Procreate: To conceive a child through sexual intercourse with the opposite sex. The most important aspect of being a biological father is the bonding that may be created by the child being your own flesh and blood. By being in a child's life from birth is an advantage of truly caring for the child unconditionally and providing an endless supply of Kool-aid. Men don't necessarily have to be a biological father, or be in a child's life since birth to be an effective Kool-aid provider. As well, a biological father may run out of Kool-aid, and stop being the male role model that every family should have. To avoid this, consider LRSD below as a guide to actions of Manhood.

LRSD	
Love	Unconditional caring for their wellbeing and comforting attitude during difficult times
Respect	Consistently treat them as human beings that are worthy of your love
Support	Be present with encouragement during their victories in life by being happy for their happiness, and being sad for them during their sadness
Discipline	A fair and consistent structure of rules that allow the family members to know their responsibilities to love, respect and support their family, their community and themselves

Due to the history of slavery, institutional discrimination and financial hardships, the African American culture has created an element of dysfunction that has left many families broken. Even if you are a product of a broken home, you still have an obligation to your ancestors and your future generations to break any cycle of negativity. In this book is the understanding of why, and the description of how you can make a positive difference throughout your life. The challenge is there, the decision is yours. Your philosophy of life can be a destructive one, or a positive one.

What do you want to put into life, what do you want to get out of life?

Manhood within friendships Currently, a large percentage of African American men use a friend based manhood definition; as opposed to a family based manhood definition. Each man should ask himself which group is more important to him, his friends or his family? If you disregard your family to appease your friends, this is a major flaw that is one of the reasons African Americans have some destructive habits. The purpose of this book is to encourage the African American culture to use a family based definition of manhood. In other words, manhood should not be determined by your group of friends, it should be determined by your mother, father, sister and grandparents. True manhood causes a man to place his family above his friends. Ego, cause a man to place his friends above his family.

Manhood pact

What if you and your group of friends decided together to all become men in manhood rather than men in ego? How should you start that in your circle of friends? Make a set of rules, and discuss how to maintain and reinforce the rules.

Your manhood pact rules should answer to the question: "How does a man provide an endless supply of Kool-aid?"

Dr. Sampson Davis, Dr. George Jenkins and Dr. Rameck Hunt are three African American Doctors who made a Manhood pact while in school to encourage and support each other to become successful men. If a gang can be powerful in negativity, a group can be more powerful in prosperity. (See the book The Pact by the three doctors)

EXAMPLE MANHOOD PACT RULES

1. Encourage the group to L.R.S.D.

2. Keep your ego in check

3. Associate with "good people" and disassociate with "bad people"

4. Develop individual plans to obtain knowledge and be successful

5. Respect humanity

6. Seek elders to give the group positive information or answers to questions the group may have.

7. Respect women

8. Discourage activities that lead to crime

Activity: You are a Skyscraper

Law of thermodynamics

As a MANager who MANages a household, parents should understand the first law of thermodynamics. This law states that there is a set amount of energy in the world and that energy can not be created nor destroyed, but it can only be transferred to different forms. The reason why this is important for household MANagement is because one's responsibilities to effectively lead a family are to monitor and change the energy in the home. If there is a build-up of a lot of negative energy, everyone may have contributed to this build-up, but it is the head of the household's responsibility to change this negative energy into positive energy.

The skill to meet negative energy at the front door and change it into positive energy as it enters your house is a good skill to help a MANager to protect and provide for the family. This is a function of patching holes in family member's cups. Through educating the other members of the house, or encouraging them when they have a lot of negative energy, an effective leader can change that negative energy into a positive learning experience, hence the role of educator.

Knowledge vs. Ignorance

Knowledge is light, and ignorance is darkness. As the educator of the family, one is responsible for creating light so that the family can see, instead of living in the darkness of not understanding. Knowledge encourages positive emotions, and discourages negative emotions. As well, the opposite is true; ignorance encourages negative emotions and discourages positive emotions. The fear of the unknown, being afraid of the dark, not wanting to venture outside of your comfort zone, are all like shackles on the legs of slaves. Yet the major difference is; now we hold the key to unlock our minds and rid ourselves of fear and ignorance.

> Do you like my jewelry?
>
> Well…actually, that's not jewelry that you are wearing.
>
> Those are shackles.

Self preservation vs. sacrifice

Self preservation is the protection of oneself from harm or destruction. It is the instinct for individual preservation and the innate desire to stay alive. Each person has the choice to do, or not to do things that preserve their well being or way of life. Yet the one flaw in self preservation in a family setting is that,

"One 's self is not supposed to be the #1 priority"

As the MANager of a family, the preservation of "self" is secondary to the preservation of those family members that you are responsible for.

To sacrifice is to do without, or give up something of personal value for the benefit of your future or the benefit of others. This is the most challenging aspect of family leadership. Sacrifice is automatically expected when building a family. If you do not expect to sacrifice, or are unwilling to sacrifice some of your initial wants and desires, you will eventually fail your family.

As a man makes the decision to be the head of a household and hold himself responsible for the family members, he must try to understand what he has to sacrifice and what he plans to gain for that trade. If he remains focused on the benefits gained by building a strong family structure, he will be better suited to sacrifice other desires. A man that fails to sacrifice is a man who lost sight of the goal of family.

The Value of Manhood

What is the value of manhood?
And how is that value determined?

There are many ways to determine a fake manhood. There are things such as, how much money a man makes, how many houses, cars and jewelry they own. As well, many men in the African American culture falsely determine their sense of manhood by how many women or children they have (or have had). Yet we must remember that the value of manhood is not determined by a man himself, or his male friends who may only encourage and support in a pact, but the true determinant is how he treats his family. Using this measurement, we can see that material wealth is only good if it is used to benefit (not spoil) a man's family. Thus material wealth is to be used to obtain true manhood, but it in its self does not determine manhood.

Integrity

Material wealth can come and go over time. But if a man loses his wealth, his manhood can remain in tact. What defines a man can rarely be taken away from him. To define a man, one must look at what he does. By judging how his words match his action, his integrity is shown. Integrity is a word that every boy should know, because without integrity, manhood is impossilble to obtain.

The History of the Pimp & Playa

Traditionally within the Westernized cultures, men have taken the role of provider and protector of their families. This role was at the core of a man's pride. If a man is unable to provide for his family, his place in the household and his manhood may be questioned. The role of provider/protector is a learned tradition. This role is passed down from father to son. Yet in the history of the African American, the ability to teach this role was hindered by the institution of slavery.

During slavery, the African man was stripped of his ability to provide or protect his family. The institution of slavery was intentionally crafted in a way to remove the man's ability to provide, due to his being forced to work for no wages without the power to dictate his families choices. His ability to protect his family was hindered due to the slave masters assertion of power and control over the lifestyle choices of the enslaved family.

Overall, the African American family was strong and tightly nit because of the common struggle. They understood that they had to live and work together in order to survive, even though there was a constant challenge of roles and a building of "self-hate" that was learned from the slave master. Along with this, they had to endure the general population of Americans that looked down upon African Americans as less than human, niggers.

As African Americans gained their freedom from slavery and began to migrate North in search of better opportunities, they began to populate Urban cities, where overcrowding and urban poverty grew. They struggled to better define their male and female roles, while dealing with economic depression, discrimination and self-hate. These facts lead to the mentality of the 20th century "Pimp Game."

The popularity of the urban Pimp is a result of high unemployment among urban men. Yet the lifestyle of the Pimp in manipulating women into degrading themselves in order to support him financially is the opposite of Manhood as defined in this book; as well as being counterproductive in being the provider/protector. Having a woman walk the streets and sell her body for money to bring to a man is not a traditional exhibition of manhood. So the men who chose this lifestyle, embellished in flashy clothes, over-the-top jewelry and expensive cars. The reason for the flashiness was to create a false extension of a non-existent manhood. Pimps actually exploited their own women with great detriment to their own communities.

This community of people had to remove the guilt that may have been associated with the act, and replace it with a false sense of pride and ego. This pride and ego within the pimp game has become normal. The guilt was easily replaced due to the fact that we were the sons and daughters of slaves, so to diminish the rights and freedoms of an African Americans was an American custom. The only thing that changed was the skin color of the master.

A Playa is an urban slang term derived from the term "playboy", a man who has physical relationships with multiple women on an on-going basis. This Playa lifestyle has been glorified by many American sub-cultures, yet African Americans have embraced this activity in a broader sense, regardless of the tremendous negative affect on society. The difference between a Pimp and a Playa is that Pimps earn money through exploiting women, while a Playa exploits for personal emotional gains. Within the last 20 years, the words Pimp and Playa have become interchangeable, but both represent a man that chooses to use multiple women for superficial reasons while feeling guiltless regarding any damage to the spirit of the multitude of women involved.

To this day, there is a large percentage of the urban male population that, due to a lack of academic success, disenfranchisement and felonious activity are unable to build a solid and stable foundation to house the responsibility of a family. Hence these men tend to not be the true providers of the household. They struggle for power and comfort in a household that is truly being secured by a more educated, more mature and more independent woman. These men tend to walk with a swagger, have their chest out and lean to the right while driving. These acts are like the flashiness of the "old school pimp", they serve as tactics to mask the truth of inadequate manhood.

The playa mentality may become a lifestyle that is difficult to break. Once you are in a relationship with someone worthy, you want to be able to change your lifestyle to cater to your partner's emotional well-being.

Bucket of women

Each man should develop a bucket that they mentally place women in. The more types of women in the bucket, the more mature the man. As a teenager or young adult male, their may be a very few amount of women that you would claim "I would not have relations with that type of women." The smaller the list of types of women in your bucket, the more willing you are to have superficial relationships with various types of women. The process of maturing into strong manhood is understanding what you want and need out of relationships; as well as understanding what types of women do not fit that description. Then you'll need the discipline to not waist or risk your time on unnecessary relationships. Mature men focus on not exploiting women by obtaining as many women as possible, as the socially immature playa may choose. That would be catering to your Ego, as apposed to creating a strong sense of Manhood.

As a man gets older and more mature, his list of women that he would not engage in an intimate relationship with should grow. This represents having control over the type of people you allow into your life. The more you do that, the better position you will be in to find a suitable partner to be in a relationship with. As well, you will become a better partner. A married man has agreed to place all other women in his bucket. The bigger your bucket is before marriage, the easier the marriage lifestyle will be regarding other women.

The definition of manhood as stated in this book is crafted in a way that creates the healthy development of a culture. Pimps and Playas are not living a lifestyle of true manhood that builds families, they are living a life less than manhood that destroys families.

> **Topic for discussion**
>
> What different types of women are available? Which would you avoid and why?

Hustler

A hustler is a person that earns money in a non-traditional, often times illegal way. He may be a business man that doesn't obtain the proper government approval, and he does not pay taxes on his earnings. The Hustler mentality has been born out of basic survival needs. As jobs were not available, people turned to alternative ways to earn money. As people were un-educated and un-qualified to earn a living the traditional way, they learned to supply products and services to meet or create a need in the community.

The main reason why the activities of the hustler are not traditional is due to the direct harm that activity causes society. Either the products were unsafe, or it was unfair to traditional businesses, or there was no (tax) public benefit received by the government. Hustlers tend to not want to pay taxes, or to compete fairly with businesses that would normally not hire them in the first place. But regarding the harm that some of these products caused the public, hustlers must have an "I don't care" mentality.

Topic for discussion
Are all Hustles illegal or immoral?

The "I don't care" mentality is basically a guilt free feeling about the harm of doing things immoral. This quality that most Hustlers need to posses has grown throughout the urban communities. Left with little options, a sub-culture within the African American community has grown more and more guiltless regarding what type of impact their hustle has on the world. The result is animal like existence of kill or be killed. This breeds the literal interpretation of the lifestyle of a "nigga." Education and compassion is the only way to correct the "nigga" lifestyle.

With education and compassion, African Americans can take the energy of the hustler and make a legitimate career. With more African American minds creating legitimate businesses, the more employment opportunities exist. The more legitimate and moral the ways one makes money, the longer he will have and enjoy money.

Activity: The hats we wear

Institutionalization

African Americans make up 13% of the U.S. population, yet they make up 30% of the U.S. prison population. The U.S. prison system is the undisputed modern day descendant of slavery. Many men of today say that they would have refused to be a slave back in the 1700's and 1800's. Yet those slaves had no choice. In most instances, imprisonment is voluntary. Typically, you knowingly do something wrong in order to be imprisoned.

The "slavery lifestyle" is an option that can be taught using a "slave mentality." The first choice is when a child is not given or does not take advantage of educational opportunities. The second choice is usually one's choice of friends. The last decision to volunteer for modern day slavery is the choice of a life of crime. Once a person has a felony on his/her record, they not only have to do the time in prison, but they must live with the limits the title of ex-convict holds. They are permanently labeled a second-class citizen with lesser rights and freedoms to be successful in life.

Some sub-cultures have glorified the lifestyle of institutionalization, simply because in some groups, the biggest hustler is glorified or looked up to. Most hustles come to an end, and many hustlers go to jail for their crimes. Once they are released, they do as the pimp did, and make everyone believe that lifestyle is cool, positive or admirable. Yet again, an example of a false sense of manhood.

| Self-hate |

Self-hate is an emotion which creates carelessness in ones own personal or cultural well being. Pimping, drug sales and child abandonment can only be a viable option for a community when there is a lack of respect for the group that is being victimized. African Americans have exhibited a level of ruthless self-hate unmatched by any other American sub-culture. Rooted in the institution of American slavery and continued well after slavery, the hate shown towards African Americans has been internalized, as they began to hate themselves as a people. If all other groups stopped hating African Americans, it would do no good for the African American community unless African Americans stopped hating themselves.

The corrective action in eliminating self-hate is not just stopping gang violence, or drug sales in the African American community, but it would also include trusting and believing in one another, and making an effort to support one another with brotherly love (Ma'at)

Activity: Generational Linkage

Manhood Concluded

A part of being a man is the ability to make your own decisions in life. The principles that you believe in will dictate your outcome in life. If you glorify negativity and treat people with disrespect, then you will suffer the consequences. If you devalue education and never try to accomplish anything great in life, you will never be great. This country is set up so that those who don't believe in themselves will never have happiness, and those that do put forth effort, will win in the end.

In order to win, a man must understand and practice Ma'at and integrity. He must be willing to do what's right instead of do what is popular. That is a part of being your own man as opposed to being someone else's flunky, nigga or slave. The United States is not about individuals, it is about groups. You will rise or fall with your group of friends or family. You must find or create a group with high standards and never let your failures define you. Always get back up after falling and continue to press forward for something greater. That "never give up" attitude of hope and faith is the ONLY difference between success and failure.

Which are you?

CHAPTER NOTES

Thoughts, questions and solutions:

_____

_____

_____

_____

_____

_____

Personal challenges covered in the chapter:

_____

_____

_____

_____

Potential ways to create change in my life/house/community:

_____

_____

_____

_____

_____

_____

_____

Action plan and accountability follow up dates:

_____

_____

_____

_____

_____

_____

_____

_____

_____

Womanhood

"These are the women in my life, my mother, momma Kay, the girl's godmothers, girlfriends of mine who help me shuttle and keep me held up"

"That is the dilemma women face today. Every woman that I know, regardless of race, education, income, background, political affiliation, is struggling to keep her head above water. We try to convince ourselves that somehow doing it all is a badge of honor, but for many of us it is a necessity and we have to be very careful not to lose ourselves in the process"

Michelle Obama

Womanhood is a concept that encompasses the roles and emotions that women possess. A woman is an adult female human. The suffix hood, represents the state of being.

For the sake of this book, when the word "hood" is used in conjunction with the words man, woman or child, it represents the role and expected actions within the context of a family. The role woman should play regarding family is the topic of this chapter. We will discuss the various levels of womanhood, as well as determine other options outside of acting in womanhood. Obtaining a sense of womanhood begins when a girl's body begins to change to prepare for womanly duties. This can occur as early as 8 years old. Legally, at the age of eighteen womanhood reaches a milestone. Once a girl steps away from her childhood by taking on womanly roles within her family or in the world, womanhood is in full effect. However, the type of womanhood may still be in development.

Womanhood has been defined in three different ways: as a state or time of being a woman; the combination of qualities thought to be an appropriate representation of woman; and lastly, sisterhood, which is women operating collectively.

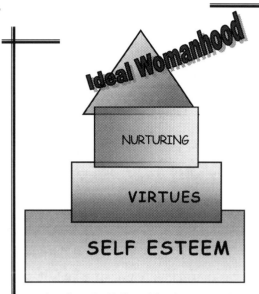

The first building block to creating the "Ideal Womanhood" is Self Esteem. With a strong and positive self image, a woman can stack a good set of Virtues on top. After a woman determines her virtues, she can then begin to play a roll in relationships, which represents her ability to nurture. At the top of these building blocks, the world can witness what type of woman she is. The more positive the blocks, the more Ideal the womanhood.

It is difficult to convince any female over the age of 18 that she has not entered womanhood. Yet it is not worth arguing the fact that women possess various levels of desirability regarding becoming a wife, mother, lover and friend.

THE BUILDING BLOCKS

SELF ESTEEM

What a person feels about their value or worth as an individual. This is mostly determined by other people around you. The first builder of your self esteem was your mother whom you were connected to by an umbilical cord. She fed you your first impression of who you were. Once the umbilical cord was cut, you still needed to be connected to people to understand who you were in this world. So you immediately started to attach yourself to various people by a spiritual umbilical cord. Your mother, father, siblings, friends and extended family all are connected to you through a spiritual umbilical cord. Each of these individuals push thoughts, feelings and emotions through this cord which is ultimately absorbed within you. So your self esteem (or self image) is the sum of all that has been fed into you by the people who "love you." Therefore these people may be the cause of the level of your self esteem. Or you may have rejected and overridden their information and created your own level of self esteem. We all have the inner strength to ignore information being pushed upon us, rather negative or positive. We can choose to think less of ourselves even when others are telling us that we are worthy, and this works in the opposite direction as well. We have the ability to ignore negative information and believe in ourselves. People may reject you or not give you the love and acknowledgment that you deserve. If this is the case, you must use the inner strength that you have to overcome the negative opinions in your life. Self esteem is so important to every person that you have to find a way to build it and protect it so that you can grow to be all that you are meant to be in this world.

Women with high self esteem are more likely to be successful in pursuing education, career, and happiness. They tend to suffer less emotional damage from personal relationship break-ups. In essence, self esteem is inner strength.

VIRTUES

A set of personal principles that a person sets for themselves. Those virtues tell if a woman commands respect, or is willing to be disrespected. The word virtue is also interchangeable with words such as morals, ethics and class. So if a woman suffers from low self esteem, caused by the people she is spiritually connected to, she is at a higher risk of allowing herself to be abused and mistreated by others. She is relatively more susceptible to becoming a Hoe *(as defined below)*. Conversely, if a woman was fed positive emotions and has high self esteem, she is more likely to be unwilling to tolerate disrespect on many levels.

A woman's virtues will dictate what type of woman she is. Once positive virtues are established, she may be ready to enter into meaningful relationships with other people. Prior to this knowledge of self, relationships are basically "practice." Throughout our school years, we practice relationships. Yet as we change, we can out grow our relationships. Some friends grow with us and remain friends, and some we have to disassociate with simply because they are heading in a different direction. The decision to change in various directions can be our own, or they can be forced upon us. If we make up our minds ourselves, we are of strong Will. If we are not of strong Will, we will tend to follow what "everyone else" is doing. This "follower mentality" often times creates many problems. In lower socioeconomic communities there are many negative elements or traps that a person can fall into. This is why being strong willed and not depending on others for your self esteem or virtues is very important to success.

Understanding one's self before entering into a meaningful relationship is important because, at that point, a woman will know how and why she will nurture each relationship. Prior to that understanding, a woman may nurture the wrong people for the wrong reasons in the wrong way. This outcome is a waste of time and results in hurt feelings; hence meaningless relationships in the long run. There is no set age where this understanding one's self happens. One can be very young, or one may never accomplish this understanding and live a life filled with meaningless relationships. Floating aimlessly in different harmful relationships year after year is very unhealthy to the spirit of a woman. The difficulty is that most women, who understand, *know*. And the women that don't understand, *think they know*. Ignorance is blissfully painful.

NURTURING	1. The broad definition is providing nourishing sustenance with the purpose of feeding, training, educating or cultivating. 2. The womanly/motherly definition that this chapter focuses on is the act of

providing nourishing sustenance within a relationship for the purpose of growing a stronger bond of interdependence, <u>mutual</u> respect and love.

Women instinctively nurture. The desire and ability to communicate with a most vulnerable baby who can not speak, in order to bring the baby comfort in a healthy loving way is an innate talent within little girls that are naturally attracted to dolls. The additional levels of sensitivity and the ability to communicate affection is a necessity to the survival of the human race. This God given talent and duty of baring and caring for a child is the most honored role anyone could ever perform. To not honor thy mother and thy wife is arguably the biggest crime against humanity.

To nurture others is the purpose of women. As it is the responsibility of men to protect and provide, it is the women's role to bring comfort to her family. This is the natural exchange between the sexes in order to supply all the needs of each family

> **Topic for discussion**
>
> Discuss the many ways a woman can nurture herself.

member. Even the best of women forget one essential part of nurturing; she must first and frequently nurture herself. She must give herself the self love, the self respect, and hold herself accountable to being a great person with a healthy level of independence. This creates confidence, which is the stuff people can feel radiate from a woman who knows how to nurture herself. From that standpoint, she will be ready to nurture others in a healthy exchange.

If a little girl's self esteem is damaged by those in which she is spiritually connected with, she may lose the ability to positively establish virtues that allow her to effectively nurture her adult relationships. This is a crime, not only against the little girl, but also against the woman she will become, and the child she will eventually bare and the husband she may never marry or eventually divorce.

The perfect balance of self respect, caring judgment and sensitivity, packaged in an attitude that is attractive to most males and females (sisterhood) of all ages. These qualities cause all people to find comfort and admiration, which ultimately creates personal growth.

THE CIRCUMSTANCES

ABUSE

Criminals against the African American community that have gone unpunished and unashamed are rampant within the African American culture. Some take advantage of the most vulnerable people while they are in the position to protect. They violate their duty due to their selfish unwillingness to control their urge for power. Some are placed on a pedestal and given a microphone and a recording contract to propagate the demise of the African American people. By degrading the African American woman and belittling her essential role in our future success, we seal our fate into a downward spiral of mental incarceration. The hyper-sexual context of this lifestyle is identified by the lyrical content of the cultural music. Yet the source of the problem is the disconnect between African American men and women. Slavery and institutional racism may have initiated this pattern, but African Americans themselves have not been able to respond appropriately and effectively to address the problem. They currently continue the problem of not being willing to commit to a relationship and protecting each others emotional well being. Instead many within relationships experience mental, emotional, physical and sexual abuse.

In America, child molestation and sex crimes have taken a second priority to the first priority of personal liberties. From priest, to bishops, to uncles, we have sat by while this practice goes unchecked and unresolved. Many mature adults understand this destructive power, but this is only after they have ignorantly fallen prey to its fact, and now they use their emotional baggage as an excuse to neglect the obligation to act against such a massive injustice. These sexual and abusive exploits are offenses against the victim's ability to develop strong building blocks to both Ideal Womanhood and Manhood.

It is estimated that 1 in every 4 women suffer an abusive childhood. Yet this only represents documented or admitted cases. For every one revealed case, there may be two cases that are not revealed. Many people don't know that they were abused because they believe their experiences to be normal, or that it was what they wanted. Yet elders have a responsibility to monitor and protect the young and vulnerable. We must hold them accountable for their actions, and then we must forgive and heal.

FATHERLESSNESS

In reference to the Manhood chapter, there are many forces working against African American men that assist the men in having excuses not to take their rightful place in the household. Yet this separation from the family is not properly discouraged culturally. The void that an absent father creates has the most profound affect on the self esteem of their daughters. The father-daughter relationship is critical to the development of a young woman. As her first male/female relationship, he is the most important source of self esteem. His relationship with her will have a large impact on her relationships with all men in her younger years. As more and more girls are raised without their fathers playing a positive role in their lives, women are left to fill the void. A present father who is not engaged in positively and effectively raising his children is similarly harmful. Young girls in this situation need to be taught about this void and the different ways to resolve these voids in a positive healthy manner. Yet the problem is that to fully understand this concept takes a level of maturity that most young girls have not reached. In other words, you may be in a situation that you do not understand. You are a victim of a broken home, and that makes you more likely to be a victim to a number of men in the future. The challenge that you face with this information is that you have to find the inner-strength, courage and wisdom to refuse being a victim.

I will not be a victim!

Being told or discovering that you may have a void created by an absent father is step one. Step two is to admit and accept this void. Your initial reaction may be to deny any shortcomings. You may tend to provide excuses or examples of women with fathers that had voids, or women without fathers that seemingly had no voids. Yet understand, it is better to acknowledge the possibility, than to ignore the reality. The third step is to be very careful of what type of men you allow into your life. Take your time and allow him to display his true character and intentions prior to letting him in too close. Immature men tend to be lion predators. Mature men tend to be protectors and providers. As a woman of low self esteem you are like a wounded deer in the wild that will be consumed by lions. No one can give you the needed strength to survive. You must seek it, take it and own it.

"Pain makes you bitter or better"
Bishop T.D. Jakes

THE OPTIONS

HOE   HOUSEWIFE

HOE AND HOUSEWIFE are (for the sake of this books discussion) two extreme ends of a spectrum of female lifestyles. Most men appreciate both ends of the spectrum at various times in their lives. As well, many women adopt and change the various lifestyles throughout their lives. The constant sliding on this scale is what makes relationships very complicated. A Hoe lifestyle is one that exhibits a low value on relationship commitment and the institution of marriage. A Housewife lifestyle is one that exhibits the very opposite. A hoe does not necessarily disrespect her body frequently, but more importantly, she is likely to, knowingly interfere in a relationship involving two other people. A housewife is not necessarily married. Yet given her lifestyle of relationship respect, she is considered "wife material", which means men will consider her for marriage at a higher rate than the alternative lifestyle. This distinction is very important to the success of the institution of marriage, and family stability overall. A community's [or culture's] rate of successfully building strong families is closely tied to the percentage of Hoes vs. Housewives that make up that population.

The more Hoes that involve themselves with men who are "committed" to another person, the more damage suffered by relationships in general. Yet the more women who hold back on giving "husband benefits" to boyfriends and casual acquaintances, the better off the culture/society will be regarding how their families are built. Sex is only one aspect of relationships, but sexual lifestyle dictates morals, discipline, strength of selfhood and emotional baggage. Many people will agree that trust is the single most important characteristic within a successful relationship. Hence, character and the respect for boundaries are very important.

SLUT

The term Slut, initially termed "*slutte*", comes from Middle English in the 1400's and meant dirty, untidy or slovenly woman. It still has kept the crux of its meaning in today's society as a pejorative term, typically referring to a female who is sexually promiscuous. Closely related to a prostitute, the difference is that prostitutes are promiscuous for economic consideration. These two terms are similar to the gender specific terms pimp and player, as referenced in the Manhood chapter.

The commonality of these four terms is that most people outside of this group will agree that something is wrong emotionally with the people within this group. Without judging the morality of the lifestyle, we can judge the effects on society these lifestyles manifest. Generally:

- The reduced emotional and financial support to the offspring of this group.
- The potential social and mental damage suffered by this group in the long term.
- The potential physical damage and aging suffered by this group.

BOUNDARIES

There are two relationship boundaries that if crossed with another person outside of the relationship, may create problems. The first is an emotional connection, where a person in a relationship feels deeply for another person other than the person they are in a relationship with. The second boundary is sexual connection. In both cases the offended party in the relationship may feel one or both of the following:

Jealous: The feeling that an energy that is supposed to be theirs is being received by another person.

Insecure: The fear of losing the future benefits that the relationship promises.

How a person uses the 14 emotions from chapter 2 determines their character/personality. An over dependence on jealousy creates insecurities that can quickly become a negative character trait if not managed to a healthy level. Frequent bad experiences or low self esteem, creates insecurities. That person becomes less attractive to be in a relationship with. The more beautiful you are on the outside, the more people you will attract. Yet the less beauty you possess on the inside, the more people will leave you. Just as you take pride in your exterior, you need to take pride in your interior by respecting and protecting yourself.

LIFESTYLE CHOICES

This discussion is important to all young women of today because each will all have the option to adapt any number of these lifestyles. Each woman will also encounter or be affected by women of different lifestyles. The important lesson to gain here is the general reasons why women take on such lifestyles, as well as the impact on society these lifestyles have. In reviewing the building blocks of Ideal womanhood, along with the 14 emotions discussed in chapter 2, you may be able to imagine what goes wrong with a young lady as she develops into her own lifestyle and womanhood.

Sex is only one aspect of relationships, yet a person's sexual lifestyle is a strong indicator of their level of morals, discipline and selfhood. An inappropriate sexual lifestyle may create emotional baggage that affects ones ability to develop successful relationships. By managing your own sexual lifestyle and paying attention to others sexual lifestyle you may be able to avoid costly emotional drama and spiritual trauma.

SISTERHOOD

 A major component of Ideal womanhood is the practice of respecting other woman's relationships rather than competing with them for relationships. This respect is also expressed by supporting one another through life's trials and tribulations. As a leader, you will be responsible for those who follow you. As a follower, you will be responsible for your own actions, regardless of who you may have followed. You are accountable for your own actions and how those actions affect others. Regardless of how old a person may be, each of us has a childhood tendency to test the boundaries of our relationships. Our friends may test the strength of our friendships. In these cases we must stand firm to what is acceptable, yet not be too quick to give up on the friendship. The strength to support one another is a key element to sisterhood. This is difficult to do without being overly judgmental. We must attempt to balance what type of behavior we will tolerate, with what behavior is unacceptable. A strong sisterhood is built upon an appropriate balance of the two while avoiding being hypocritical.

Problems look much easier to resolve as you view them from the outside. Yet from within a situation, you are not only dealing with the occurrences, but you also have the emotional connection to deal with. When in sisterhood, consoling and supporting is complicated due to the different perspectives. When supporting within sisterhood, compassion and empathy is detrimental for sisterhood to flourish.

BITCH

A bitch literally means female dog. As this word is used to describe a women, it is to demine her actions. Acting like a bitch is acting unladylike, or acting less than she would in womanhood. People often use this derogatory word to describe a woman who is "overly" aggressive, nasty or un-submitting. Women often believe that these character traits are required in order to accomplish her goals or to protect herself from others who may attempt to take advantage of her. Yet the word bitch is used in the same way that the word nigger was used by racist white Americans to demean African Americans.

In modern times, African Americans have adapted these demeaning words and use them as a term of endearment. Yet there is a debate as to if these words still have a negative effect on the subconscious of the people it is used against, regardless of the intent. Some women call their female friends this negative derogatory word while in casual conversations. The accurate application of Ma'at by a person will create an unwillingness to use either of these words to describe anyone. The use of the word is very unladylike. People of a higher class do not use this word, and the high class people who do use the word, can stop using it if they choose to. So the test becomes, "can you stop using the term?"

DEGRADING LYRICS IN MUSIC

Many women enjoy music with degrading lyrical content.

Lisa: I like that music, the rapper is not talking about me, so it doesn't matter.

Kelly: But by buying that music you are supporting and promoting the lifestyle of degrading women. So more and more, young boys grow up thinking that women don't deserve respect. Then when you are 45 years old and can't find a "good man"

Topic for discussion

What are some of the negative ways that woman degrade one another?

What are some of the positive things that woman can do to build a stronger sisterhood?

Activity: You are a Skyscraper

MS. INDEPENDENT

Within the American culture and in the African American community especially, women are taking on larger rolls within the household, such as primary provider and sole provider. More and more women are either electing to or being forced to live a life as a single woman or a single parent. This trend is determined by many factors in today's society, but nevertheless, women still should choose a lifestyle that is not only best for them, but should also take into consideration how their lifestyle will effect their family and their society.

The positive aspect of being Ms. Independent is a woman who is capable of managing her affairs without much assistance from others. She is strong willed and confident in completing the tasks of life. The negative aspect of being Ms. Independent is the perception that she has set her standards too high regarding what type of life partner she will submit too. There may be a few

Independent women who do not have the desire to be in a relationship where they would have to submit. Yet the majority of women would like to have someone they deem responsible enough to relinquish some of their responsibilities to. By having higher standards than most men in her circle, she vows to be Ms. Independent for as long as it takes.

How does being Ms. Independent effect Ideal womanhood? Ms. Independent has yet to find a partner that she is willing to give 20% of her responsibilities to, in exchange for 20% of his responsibilities. She keeps her responsibilities for herself. Remember "hood" in this book represents relationships with the family. Thus, within ideal womanhood there are significant responsibility-sharing. To swap responsibilities according to different talent and skill levels is an advantage. Yet the point of this book is to encourage men to be worthy of women with high standards. Ms. Independent is upholding the values and expectations that we all need. Yet potential partners need to meet expectations of mutual respect, love and effort. This ideal situation will make for a better family environment for future generations.

> **Topic for discussion**
>
> What are some of the factors that contribute to women having to take on a more independent role?

VARIATIONS ON THIS SCALE

High class, low class, no class, Ideal womanhood, slut... All of these words are labels to describe the actions (lifestyle) of an individual. The only thing stopping a person from changing their lifestyle is themselves. We should all want to do better, be better and have better. Once you stop wanting to improve, you have reached your highest level of esteem, by placing your own boundary upon yourself.

Women and men's preference tends to change over time regarding the morals that they hold or demand from people they deal with. Yet no one can date alone, it takes not only a partner, but an entire dating pool of people. Accordingly, if the pool has many people with low standards, it becomes difficult to find a person of high moral character, and it is more difficult to be a person of high moral character. This causes pools to generally change in a negative direction.

The general American culture, as well as the African American culture (at a faster pace), has been in moral deterioration since the 1960's (with the exception of acts of racism). The marriage rates have been in continuous decline, the divorce rates and single parent household rates have been consistently on the rise. The importance of morals and family structure is at question. The direction society should take is at question. Many people believe in the philosophy of "live and let live." This perspective is based on the idea that people should be free to do what ever they want to do as long as it is not breaking any laws. With that philosophy, this book is a moot point. Yet the true focus of this book is to create a thought process in each individual about how and why they interact with others.

COMPETITION FOR ATTENTION

In the African American community there has been many cultural factors that have developed due to slavery and economic disadvantage. The lack of opportunity for African American men as they seek to secure the ability to provide for a family has left many African American men disenfranchised (unwilling to participate in social, economic, political arenas). Disenfranchisement creates low peeks of manhood (lack of success). In other words; personal, social and career opportunities are limited. So a disenfranchised man will never live up to his potential greatness, as discussed in the Manhood chapter. Disenfranchisement is also discussed in the following Community chapter. However, this disenfranchisement directly affects a person's ability to be successful within a family environment as well. African American men historically have been more directly affected by disenfranchisement than African American women. Yet African American women have been indirectly affected by the shortage of men who are willing and able to be the provider or life partner that they require.

The disenfranchised man often times is not equipped to give a women all that she needs in a relationship. This lowers his desire to commit to a long-term relationship. Men who are successful, on the other hand, are at a higher demand from women given their status in life. This extra attention from many women makes committing to a long-term relationship difficult for the "successful" man.

SHORTAGE OF GOOD BLACK MEN

The definition of a "Good Black Man" for the sake of our discussion, is a man who is willing and able to live in strong manhood (Procreate, Educate, Protect & Provide). The shortage of Good Black Men, rather it be actual or falsely perceived by women is creating more competitiveness between women for the "few good men" that are available to them. As more and more men choose lifestyles not based on commitment, women are faced with three options:

1. Adapt by lowering their standards and relationship expectations
2. Become more competitive or aggressive in obtaining one of the few "good black men" that exist
3. Become Ms. Independent and not force a relationship

The initial problem of this paradigm is firstly the man's inability to take his place in the household. The second problem is women's decreased ability to live up to the standards of "Ideal Womanhood." Regardless of the root of the problem, both men and women have specific personal issues to focus on correcting. The only solution to this problem is for both/all men and women to make asserted efforts for self improvement.

As young girls mature into adult women, their perception of what a desirable man is, changes. As women's needs grow over time, thus too will their expectations. So happiness between men and women is highly dependent upon the men's ability and willingness to grow as a provider to meet the ever growing needs of the family. The average young person is unaware of this fact.

> *Have you ever woke-up one morning feeling great? You got through the entire day with a joyous feeling, and by the end of the day you think "today was a good day"? That is the feeling you should try to have everyday. That is the feeling you should have most days. If you don't have those days often, it is most likely due to a pain, hurt or uncertainty in your life. You deserve to have a good day everyday. When you start to feel that you do not deserve happiness you begin to lose* **hope and faith**. *At that point you will begin to devalue your self-worth and your esteem will suffer. If you don't feel highly of yourself, you will be more likely to disrespect your self, degrade yourself and allow yourself to deal with things that you should not deal with.*

MATURITY, PRIORITIES & VALUES

Many girls and young ladies value superficial qualities in a young man that are not true elements of manhood. As long as women appreciate things that are not life sustaining, men will pursue those things in order to attract women. Once people mature beyond superficial signs of power and respect, they may find that others who are still superficial are no longer attractive. So the difficulty is to get those who have not changed their superficial values, to reprioritize for the sake of their future. Examples of immature lifestyles that may be attractive in the short run, but unattractive in the long run:

| Class clown, ill gotten wealth, the bad boy, the star athlete |

If a young man never matures beyond the above lifestyle, then he may fail to live up to his potential in living in strong manhood, He will eventually contribute to the shortage of "good Black men."

MEN CAN NOT EXIST WITHOUT WOMEN,
& WOMEN CAN NOT EXIST WITHOUT MEN,
THUS WE SURVIVE, STRIVE OR DIE TOGETHER

Activity: Win/Win Win/Lose

THE FACETS

WOMANHOOD FEELS LIKE

We learn our perceived value by listening to the opinions of people around us. Our family, friends and associates treat us in ways that help us shape our self image. We are born with a unique personality. This personality determines how easily we will be influenced by others interacting with us. The experience in relationships with others, coupled with our personalities help us form an opinion of who we are, and who we can become. This shapes what we feel like.

Females, by nature are more expressive of their emotions. Males tend to be attracted to a lifestyle of holding in or ignoring their emotions as they mature. Yet the process of maturing is the continued understanding of why we feel what we feel and controlling our emotional responses. Each experience we encounter triggers an emotional response. Those extreme emotional responses are recorded into our long term subconscious mind. If there is a similar situation that arises in the future, it can trigger the same emotional response. This list of emotional experiences that accumulate in our subconscious will be used to determine our future happiness. By having many negative experiences, our outlook on life can be negative, simply due to the number of future experiences that will remind us of the negative past. Thus, if something negative happened to you when you were 9 years old, it can have a negative impact on you for the rest of your life.

One key element of living a happy life is to forgive. To forgive is to not hold a grudge or a bad feeling in your subconscious that can continue to haunt your happiness for years to come. Forgiving has three vital components:

54

1. Identify who offended you, or contributed to the bad experience in your life
2. Forgive them in order to release their power to cause you pain
3. Forgive yourself for what you may have done to contribute to that experience. If you hold negative feelings about yourself, your esteem will be oppressed and you will never strive for the greatness that you are capable of

We are social beings and we need others around us to validate us, encourage us and to give us a sense of self. Those people that are around you now that devalue you, discourage you and lower your sense of self are the people that may be the cause of your pain. The first step in obtaining happiness may be to change the people that are around you. Those people may be your family and are unavoidable in the near future. Though this may be true, it doesn't change the fact that you need to rid yourself of negative peoples influence over your life.

Fill your time and energy with people who believe in you; people who will encourage you, respect you and build your esteem. If you can't find them in the natural, find them in history; find them in books. There have been many African American women who have overcome great pain, suffering and abuse and triumphed. Their life's story is proof that you can accomplish greatness and Ideal womanhood regardless of your past or present. Seek those sources that are enlightening and uplifting. They will lift you.

The more you seek goodness from bad people, the more you will be hurt. You can't change people, no matter how bad you want them to change, no matter how much you want to change them.

Don't try to change people's lives, change the people in your life

If you want to truly change people's lives, you must change yourself and allow them to see your growth. Even if you must leave them behind, you must not allow others to stop your progress.

WOMANHOOD ACTS LIKE

Women by nature are nurturers. Nurture is defined by a persons caring actions within a personal relationship that is for the purpose of influencing growth, development and mutual respect. Nurturing comes natural to a woman who has not been overly damaged by her past. The first person you should nurture is YOURSELF. By focusing on your personal qualities and growing as a person of worth and value, you will be a person that is deserving of greatness from others. The best way to attract exceptional people in your life is to become an exceptional person. If you want people to contribute a lot to your relationship, you must have a lot to contribute as well.

Be careful to not give too much of yourself to people who do not deserve or reciprocate the same level of generosity. Once you build a strong sense of selfhood and self esteem, you will be more concerning and not allow people to use you. Being used continuously is to give energy and never get energy in return; the end result is that you are left drained or bitter. Ideal womanhood will not allow this.

WOMANHOOD LOOKS LIKE

How a woman dresses shows how she feels about herself. If she has low self esteem, feels ugly, or feels unworthy, it will show in her choice of clothing and how she presents herself to the world. These women tend to have extreme styles. They under-dress, over-dress or over expose themselves to either get or avoid attention. A women living in Ideal womanhood, dresses appropriately and with tasteful moderation. She never disrespects herself by dressing overly provocative, yet she takes pride in her appearance. The clothes, makeup and all the accessories that women have to enhance their beauty may be used in proper moderation by the Ideal woman.

WOMANHOOD SMELLS LIKE

The economics of female products…weaves…perfumes…nail and salon expenses is a $10 billion industry. The scent of a woman is very enticing to men, and how a woman puts her personal presentation together is very important. Yet at what expense and to what extreme a woman should go just to "feel-good about herself" is the question that should be addressed. Women often claim that they are not dressing up for others to appreciate, but they are doing it to "feel-good about themselves", so if they are doing too much, they are implying that they don't feel-good about themselves naturally.

The U.S. media and society itself dictate what beauty is. As women chase the fantasy and try to look like someone they are not, the more money and energy they spend on the superficial aspect of womanhood. Many women who go to extremes for the sake of beauty, often neglect the most important aspect of womanhood, which is what comes from inside of her. No matter how good a person makes themselves up to be by use of false products, she knows how she really looks underneath the masking products. No matter how pretty a woman may be on the outside, no one wants to ultimately end up with a person with an ugly personality as a friend or wife.

The moral of this passage is to consider inner beauty as well as external beauty, and never let the world dictate to you your worth. No matter what you look like, you must learn to love "your true self".

HOW CAN I ACCOMPLISH IDEAL WOMANHOOD?

Some readers might be able to read this section and understand it in its entirety the first time. If you feel as if you are still unclear of what ideal womanhood consists of, I suggest reading it a second time and a third if need be. As young woman, it is your obligation to not only yourself, but to woman as a whole to understand and implement what has been provided to you in this section. For the past few decades, sisterhood has been replaced with selfish, immoral, demeaning characteristics which have been a product of our individualistic society. As an African American community, it is time to reclaim what has been lost; true sisterhood and ideal womanhood. As strong, independent, beautiful, and resilient beings, you owe it to yourselves to live up to your true virtue.

An ideal virtuous woman will continue to do the following:
Demand respect
Grow from every friendly and romantic relationship
Develop the will to lead and not follow
Embrace sisterhood positively and effectively
LOVE YOURSELF FIRST

CHAPTER NOTES

Thoughts, questions and solutions:

_____

_____

_____

_____

_____

_____

Personal challenges covered in the chapter:

_____

_____

_____

_____

Potential ways to create change in my life/house/community:

_____

_____

_____

_____

_____

_____

_____

Action plan and accountability follow up dates:

_____   _____

_____   _____

_____   _____

_____   _____

_____   _____

_____   _____

_____   _____

_____   _____

FAMILY

NUCLEAR FAMILY
A family group consisting of two parents and their children, who share a household.

SINGLE PARENT
A family with only one parent in the household.

EXTENDED FAMILY STRUCTURE
A household that consist of more than two generations, and refers to the family members who extend beyond the immediate or nuclear family of parents and their children to include grandparents.

S T R U C T U R E S

SINGLE
Not married, no children

BLENDED FAMILY
A family with a step-parent

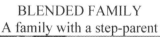

SINGLE WEEK-END PARENT

SAME SEX COUPLE

FAMILY can be defined in many ways: people you share a blood-line with, people you live with, people you share a common ancestry with, or the definition that we will refer to in this book:

> The people you have made a long term commitment to love regardless of
> what the future holds.

With this definition we can discuss who we chose to make such a commitment to, and how we carry out such commitment.

During slavery, the slave family's ability to stay together was not in their control. During that time period, it was not possible for slaves to legally marry. However, they did have ceremonies and their community respected their commitment to one another. Yet, the family was subjugated to the possibility of being torn apart at the whim of the slave master who may decide to sell the children or parents to different plantation slave owners. After the civil war, when the slaves were freed, many ex-slaves traveled the South in search of the families they were torn from.

Between 1865 and 1965, African American people were bound together by culture, discrimination, segregation and the lack of outside economic and social opportunities. Yet after major successes of the civil rights movement of the 1960's, African Americans began to popularize "Black pride." Blacks (a self imposed cultural distinction) began to indulge in the new freedoms that they won from the civil rights movement. They were less segregated and gained access to various social and economic opportunities. These opportunities were detrimental to the purities of the pre-civil rights Negro (imposed cultural distinction) culture.

There has been a drastic change in the structure of the African American family. In 1960, 70% of all Negro children were raised in a two parent household. The marriage rate was steady and divorce was rare. In the 1970's the rate of marriage began to plummet, as divorce rates sharply increased. By 1990 Black children being born to single teenage parents was at an unprecedented high and was a national concern. By 2000 the percentage of Black children raised in a two parent household was a mere 30%. As of 2008, the percentage was 38%, the African American single parent household was double that of the national average.

The largest attributors to these statistics were the Liberal revolutions of the 1960's and 1970's. Woman's liberation, the Sexual revolution, the Government's policies on welfare (The Great

Society) and the drug epidemic of the time all played major roles in the near destruction of the Black family. The purpose of this book is to bring the truth to today's youth, as they are our answer, our solution to the problems that are more than 40 years old. If our youth do not take ownership of the problems that African American people face, and create a resolution, we as a people will continue to fragment into two distinct groups.

- The Elite group, who have assimilated into mainstream culture
- The Enslaved group, who will continue to live in ignorance of the truth

Each of these groups will eventually be destroyed. The first group will destroy any commonality of a distinctive African American culture. The second group will create a permanent underclass of modern day slaves that will continue to fill substandard schools and prison systems.

Slave: One who fails to plan for or is unable to control his/her own destiny

What now?

So what is the proper family structure?	The proper family structure is which ever one produces the most emotionally stable, physically healthy and mentally capable fa
Who determines this proper family?	Each individual must determine their future by establishing a set of moral standards to live by
How do we work towards that ideal structure?	Education that defeats ignorance that creates better choices of not sharing negative emotions, but creating positive emotional experiences for others

ROMANTIC RELATIONSHIPS

A romantic relationship is a unique set of emotional experiences that one person has shared with another, which creates a desire to continue an association. Each relationship is unique due to the uniqueness of the shared experiences that manifest feelings.

THE 3 RELATIONSHIPS - Superficial | Successful | Dysfunctional

Independent relationships (Superficial) – Are relationships between two people who are independent and do not depend on each other to any great extent. These relationships tend to not last through difficult times given the ease at which each person could leave the relationship. Each person maintains their independence by not investing enough emotion or energy into the relationship to out-weight the feeling of loss in the event of a break-up.

Interdependent relationships (Successful) – Are relationships between two people who have relatively more emotions invested compared to an independent relationship. They would feel a great amount of negative emotions if the relationship were to end. The anticipation of negative emotions causes the persons to be more willing to maintain the relationship during turbulent times.

Codependent relationships (Dysfunctional) – Are relationships between two people who have an excessive amount of dependence upon one another. This dependence can be based on any type of emotion or energy. Yet the idea or feeling that "I can't live without you" or "You are what makes me happy" is also called toxic love. Toxic love is "love learned wrong." As children and others witness dysfunctional relationships, they often time copy those tendencies. This is a passing of habitual inappropriateness that must be warded off and rejected.

"Save it for marriage" A once popular statement to teenagers from parents. This statement is rapidly growing obsolete. "Save it for marriage" diminishes as the population is marrying at later and later stages in life, and perceptions change to believe that it is very difficult to find a partner worthy of marriage. Parents are now raising their children to be much more independent. This is not a cause, but an effect that perpetuates the reality that marriage is becoming less of a priority within the African American culture.

Marriage was very important to African slaves in America. Even when they were not legally allowed to marry, they would hold ceremonies and honor their vows as a community. Once the slaves were freed, many traveled many many miles in search of their families that they were separated from due to slavery. Currently 2/3 of all African American children are born into single parent households. This makes it virtually impossible to maintain the strong moral value of committing ones self to a lifemate. Children may subconsciously learn that all romantic relationships are temporary in nature, thus the attempt to make a lifelong commitment may be incomprehensible.

Lifemates – Two people, not of blood relation, who vow to utilize the majority of their life's energy for the betterment of each other.

Life's energy – The power harnessed by an individual that can be used to affect another person's emotions. This can be represented by verbal and non-verbal communication, material wealth, and emotional expressions; such as prayer, wishes, hopes and faith.

Declaration of Independence - Since the 1940's, people in the United States have been becoming increasingly independent. Starting with women moving into the workforce during World War II to replace the men who were off to war. In the 1950's households became accustom to two incomes. In the 1960's, personal freedoms were enhanced by the civil rights struggles, the women's liberation and hippie movements. The 1970's ushered in the sexual revolution and gave witness to a great increase in divorces, which either was a response to, or a catalyst of individuals becoming increasingly independent. Throughout this time people have shifted their focus from family strength, to individual strength.

Gender based expectations have diminished over this same time period. Cooking being the job of the woman, and men being the "bread winner" are no longer the expected norm. It is not uncommon to have a woman that does not cook, yet earns more than her counterpart. This eclectic mix of skill-sets creates a population of independent people that fall prey to low relationship success rates.

Human beings are social by nature. We were not meant to live alone, and we can not live up to our potential without positive social interaction that supplies positive emotions. It is important to remember the 14 emotions stated in chapter 2 when discussing romantic relationships. The purpose of romantic relationships is to enhance each person's life. If a relationship brings you more pain then pleasure, or more sadness than happiness or more despair than hope, you must question the necessity of the relationship.

During the course of a relationship, we are constantly seeking the answers to the following:

FOUR ESSENTIAL RELATIONSHIP QUESTIONS:
1. What do I need from the relationship?
2. Is the other party able and willing to supply those needs?
3. What does the other person need from this relationship?
4. Am I willing and able to supply those needs?

When a relationship does not work out, it represents the wrong answers to the questions posed.

Self-reflection: When evaluating question 3 and 4, we may learn that we are too selfish to be in a good relationship. Without self evaluation a person is bound to continue a negative pattern which leads to frequent broken promises and broken families. If we make it a point to truly investigate all four questions at the beginning, middle and end of each relationship, we will start to improve our chances of relationship success.

Self-centered: At the end of a relationship, if we focus on question 2 only, we are bound to not learn enough from that lost relationship. By only focusing on shortcomings of the other party, we tend not to address our flaws and faults. Question 1 will assist us in evaluating our expectations in relationships. If objectively analyzed we may be able to see if we have reasonable or unreasonable needs.

Unreasonable needs: This is focusing on only question 1, with an insatiable appetite or neediness. Most people with extensive needs tend to have had experiences in their lives that caused spiritual voids. Humans are social beings, we have natural voids that keep us attracted and linked to others to fulfill those needs. Without these natural voids, we would not be drawn to others and live hermit lifestyles. Yet when we suffer abuse or neglect we tend to develop coping mechanisms that are unhealthy or dangerous to our spirit and the spirit of those around us. While in relationships under this state of neediness, we may tend to demand too much from the other person. This is why the understanding and improvement of selfhood is vital to personal success.

"Many people build walls just to see who cares enough to break them down"
Unknown

A coping mechanism is something that temporarily fills a spiritual void. Many coping mechanisms do not address the cause of the void, thus the void persist and is never resolved. This leads the person to grow an additive behavior for the coping mechanism that often times creates more voids. Examples of a coping mechanism are, over dependence on others, sex, drugs and alcohol. Another common coping mechanism is emotional spite. Emotional spite is also known as bitterness or meanness. As people recognize that they are unable to fill their spiritual void, they begin to sabotage their own relationships by pushing others away. This coping mechanism is based on the persons thought that relationships do not work out anyway, so why try.

3 STEP SOLUTION

VALUE	*Realize the importance of healthy relationships to the spirit and community*
SELF EVALUATION	*Attempt to learn why you feel your feelings and why you treat people the way you do*
COMMITMENT	*Commit to respecting yourself through changing for the better, and expecting respectful behavior from those you surround yourself with*

In working closely with troubled adolescents I discovered that those that had or do engage in sexual acts do so without any awareness of a mental or emotional connection of those acts. These youth are also victims of a sex crime. The relation between sex and love is foreign or obscure to them

People today, to put it simply are screwed up. We have a million dating sites of people looking for the same thing: "a connection." However, if we have all these people looking for the same thing, why do we have these sites? Our society is so fast paced and driven for the next stimulant; whether it is waiting for our phone to buzz with a new text or someone to comment on our facebook status. All this artificial crap has seeped into the home and is destroying families.

When driving, don't look in the rear view mirror the whole time, you will crash. Look forward, glance at your past and learn from

"Divorce"
It is like a death that you must recover from

Fortress Tower vs. a bunch of little shacks

Are you building a fortress tower? Or are you building a bunch of little shacks?

Are you building with a partner, or are you building temporary shacks with a bunch of

Self preservation vs. sacrifice

Self preservation is the protection of oneself from harm or destruction. It is the instinct for individual preservation and the innate desire to stay alive. Each person has the choice to do, or not to do things that preserve there well being or way of life. Yet the one flaw in self preservation in a family setting is that,

"One's self is not supposed to be the #1 priority"

As the MANager of a family, the preservation of "self" is secondary to the preservation of those family members that you are responsible for.

To Sacrifice is to do without or give up something of personal value for the benefit of your future or the benefit of others. This is the most challenging aspect of family leadership.

MONOGAMY is a lifestyle of choosing to have only one mate/partner at any one time. This lifestyle becomes increasingly more difficult to maintain as societal morals generally diminish. Monogamy may be viewed as a large sacrifice to those that choose this lifestyle. Yet all lifestyles are a choice of pros and cons, benefits and sacrifice. However, it is important to point out that serial monogamy is just as detrimental as false monogamy.

SERIAL MONOGAMY is the willingness to commit to another person, yet for only a limited amount of time, with no real intent on ever making a lifelong commitment to anyone. False monogamy is the expressing of commitment without truly living a monogamist lifestyle. An important question that a culture or society must ask is:

Is monogamy practical, beneficial and worth pursuing?

The single lifestyle is rare in that most people would choose to be in a committed relationship with someone that they truly loved and respected. To fully embrace the single lifestyle, one would have to give up the desire of wanting a singular person to share their life with. Many in the African American community are living a "fallacious single lifestyle." This lifestyle consists of disappointment with one of two things:

- Other people's inability or unwillingness to commit to a mutually respectful relationship, or
- A deeply hidden lack of self-respect caused by their personal inability to reciprocate the minimal level of mutual respect that a relationship requires.

The single lifestyle of being fully comfortable with the choice of not sharing your life's energy with any one in particular is a growing threat to the emotional stability of society. As more and more of the population feels that life is better lived alone, they are in essence voting against other peoples ability to enhance their lives in a productive way. Where this lifestyle grows, thus too grows many societal ills.

> In a discussion with her 8th grade class, Ms. Hudson asked "who here wants to get married?" Tiffany raised her hand and spoke at the same time, "I want 2 kids!"
>
> Ms. Hudson asked, "what about a husband?" Tiffany replied, "I don't want to get married, because I won't be able to get child support."

Do you want to be a single parent on purpose?

BABY MAMA DRAMA

As well as "my baby daddy" are terms popularized within the African American community during the 1990's in response to the high incidence of single parent family structures. Remember, romantic relationships are a unique set of emotional experiences that one person has shared with another. So, to have a child with a person drastically changes your relationship. The shared parental obligation creates a unique attachment. The seriousness of raising a child is reflected in each person's expectations of the other parent. When one parent does not live up to the expectations of the other, many problems can arise. Everyone should consider the following negative affects of family separation:

- The potential personal emotional pain of not being available or not having access to your child at all times

- The potential harm that the child may be in due to the absence of both parents protection

- The emotional abandonment or separation anxiety potentially suffered by the child

- The emotionally destabilizing effect of witnessing parents dating lifestyle

- Future step-parents influence or abuse

- Reduction of financial support due to a separation of parents and maintenance of two households

The lack of team effort created in dysfunctional families has a lasting impact on the children. Certain sub-cultures of African Americans have embraced dysfunction and have created terminology that gives esteem to situations that are harmful to a community. With this current trend of immoral destabilization, a community will continue to suffer as opposed to prosper.

Can a woman raise a boy into a man alone?

LOVE VS. INFATUATION

Love is an emotion that is chosen. Infatuation or lust is a temporary love where the person ultimately chooses's not to love. Many people do not understand that love is a choice that can be built from infatuation or lust. By freely allowing love to come and go within relationships, the success rates fall drastically. Once lifemates agree to choose love over independence, they stand a chance of success.

In changing the course of negative marriage and divorce rates, "cultural emotional responses" must be trained to increase effective relationships that create emotionally stable children. With a community effort, the dating pool of positive, emotionally stable persons will increase the chances of finding a compatible lifemate without the extensive damaging dating lifestyle.

LOVE IS A CHOICE - IDEAL CULTURAL EMOTIONAL RESPONSES

In choosing to love someone, one may change the way he/she responds to his/her lifemate. A positive choice would be to always express feel-good emotions within a relationship. Feel-bad emotions should be calmly expressed for the purpose of resolving those emotions, as opposed to expressing them to hurt the other person. Hurting someone because you are hurt is an emotionally immature way of managing your emotions. This tactic rarely creates harmony or strengthens love.

In a relationship, an offended party does not choose to be hurt, yet they can choose how to express that hurt. The hurt person can act in spiteful revenge by attempting to create pain for the other person. A better option may be to act in a way that will create awareness and encourage a changed mode of operation in the other party that may have offended them. An effective relationship has an element of education and empathy through communication. People are more willing and able to share such an effective relationship if they have relatively less emotional baggage which was created by suffering an excessive amount of feel-bad emotions in the past.

The African American cultural response has always been to express your feelings as they occur. Given the enormous amount of feel-bad emotions that slave, and post-slave Negro's felt, it was difficult to withhold the expression of what ever emotion dominated them at any given time. They were required to oppress their emotions towards white racist people, while being victimized by the dominant population who did not hold back on expressing their negative feeling towards Negroes. This combination has created an African American culture that is unwilling to hold back or fake emotions within the African American community.

PROPER USE OF EMOTIONS

Faith/Trust   Believe that your lifemate's personal problems will be lifted from his/her spirit.

Passion   Always explore together and learn different things to grow together, to fight against growing apart

Enthusiasm   Be friends by appreciating your lifemates goals

Fear   Take away your desire to be single by fearing it, cherish having a lifestyle of sharing your life with someone

Guilt   Despise hurting your lifemate and avoid it as much as humanly possible

Anger   Verbally communicate frustrations to educate as opposed to overreacting with the intent to hurt back

Jealousy   Respond by being a better lifemate, to reduce their desire to share with others

Loneliness   Understand that each person needs their personal space and time apart. Balance quality-time and personal time without smothering or being so far apart that you begin to see life in different ways.

UNCONDITIONAL LOVE

Love is the most important and most powerful emotion known to man. If it is unconditional, its power is magnified. Unconditional love is what we as humans all seek. Yet for some of us, our search for this unconditional love gets so tiring that we give up on the search. At that point we tend to replace that need for unconditional love with another emotion or material possession. Love from parents serves as an example of this love, when a child feels that they do not have unconditional love from both parents, a spiritual void is more likely to develop.

Men tend to let go of the idea of unconditional love more frequently. On the other hand, women tend to be more nurturing. The ultimate goal of maternal nurturing is the result of unconditional love. In the African American community, many women will grow tired of seeking unconditional love from a romantic partner, yet they do not give up on the idea so quickly. They turn to their motherly instinct and depend on the drive to procreate and give birth to a child that will more than likely love them unconditionally. So the "internal clock" of a woman is driven by the emotional drive to seek unconditional love.

This is a grand plan, yet with more than half of all Black children being raised without their father in the home, the African American culture has developed into a people of single parents who have all but given up hope on the African American mans ability to give unconditional love. Yet they continue to have babies out of wedlock.

Unconditional love is to relationships,
what Ma'at is to selfhood,
what strong Manhood is to men,
what Ideal womanhood is to women

UNCONDITIONAL LOVE?

*Should anyone expect unconditional love, when
they are unwilling to give unconditional love?*

*How much abuse and disrespect am I supposed to tolerate? If I marry
or devote myself to this man, should I allow him to take me for granted?*

*If I give her unconditional love, and always take her back regardless
of what she does, what will stop her consistently disregarding my feelings?*

How does that work in the real world?

Unconditional love is ideal, something to aspire to. Yet when two people are committed to continually seeking stronger character, integrity and harmony (Ma'at), they can view their relationship in a spiritual light.

In a marriage there are at least three spirits, and sometimes up to five or six spirits. The husband's spirit, the wife's spirit, God, and any demonic forces that act against the marriage. If the demon is attacking the husband, the couple can give the demon a name such as infidelity, addiction or negativity. It is the wife's duty to share her feelings, it is the husband's duty to listen and acknowledge her pain and concern. He must then search his soul to muster the strength to defeat this demon quickly in order to banish this demon for the sake of his family.

Ma'at teaches to constantly work on ones self for improvement. Manhood teaches that the family's health is paramount to any one person's gratification. God promises to help defeat demons that attempt to threaten the family. The wife shall pray for the husband's strength. She shall pray for her own personal understanding and patience (faith). The husband will go to God with humility and ask for his power against the demon. The couple should not have to talk about the issue every day. They can come together and create a united front against this demon through prayer. They pray for faith, healing and deliverance that will maintain unconditional love.

We don't believe in God in my house, so that does not apply to us.
If you think that you alone are personally responsible for the outcome
of your life, then you don't need faith or hope. You will handle everything on your own. That is a great strength, especially when your life, up to this point has turned out just as you planned and desired. You are one of the lucky few that have not been tested in life...yet.

I believe wholeheartedly in God, but my wife is a non-believer
Two people need to discuss and understand each others belief systems. How do you cope with life's true challenges? How willing are you to use introspection? How willing are you to make honest attempts to change for the betterment of the family?

PARENTING - DISENGAGED PARENTING VS. DIRECTIVE PARENTING

There is a large range of parenting types. Yet for the sake of simplicity, let's review just the very most extreme ends. From this perspective, a parent can design and determine what parenting style they'd like to choose.

Disengaged parenting often occurs when a parents priorities do not allow for direct parenting. They often times are dealing with their own obsessions or issues and neglect the importance of their role within the daily lives of their children. Neglect and abuse are harsh experiences that a parent may take their children through, yet parents that abuse their children often do it out of dysfunctional or toxic love. They are overly willing to share bad-feeling emotions toward their children, while lacking the expression of good-feeling emotions. A neglecting parent shows a lack of feel-good and feel-bad emotions. The source of neglect often times is the lack of love or the existence of self hate or depression on the part of the parent.

Therapy can be an effective way to resolve some of these detrimental experiences. As African Americans become culturally more aware and excepting of therapy, their chances of breaking negative cycles increase.

Disengaged parents often times would deny such a title, because they validate their activity within their child's life when they go to their child's school and raise their voice at the counselor to show their frustration or concern (bad-feeling emotions), yet neglect to actually work with the school to devise and stick to a plan of action regarding their children's learning. Additionally, parents may go to their child's sporting events, but not join the schools Parent Teacher Association (PTA), this sends the wrong message to the children regarding priorities. As well, parents may often complain about the school system, yet fail to vote, while most local and State elections have school initiatives on the ballot. Making noise does not necessarily mean something is being said.

Directive parenting is most simply a parenting style that is very focused on the long term affect of each experience the parent exposes their children to. The larger the perspective of a child, the more options and understanding the child has. Thus parents devise a systematic way of broadening their child's perspective by exposing them to various thought processes.

How Directive Parenting works- Determining your child's future for & with them by asking yourself this question: What type of adult do I want my child to become?

Disenfranchised	Disengaged, with little if any successes in life. This person seldom sets or accomplishes goals.
Average	Blends in to the crowd of mediocrity. There is nothing special about this person. He/she has unique skills and talents just as most people, yet their full potential is never realized.
Leader	An authority figure that understands the inner workings of the average person, he/she has a commanding presence that the average person admires. This makes him/her a leader.
Innovator	Someone who looks at what is, and sees what can be. This person has the vision to make the impossible, possible. This person does not follow the crowd, a maverick that is difficult for parents to teach, but ease to identify and cultivate. Parents should focus on the 15th emotion as stated below.

STEP 1- COMMIT to the following:

1. I will not get in the way of positive development of my child
2. I will cognitively pre-determine my child's future success by having high expectations
3. I will assist and motivate my child to become a great human being
4. I will love my child unconditionally, even if he/she falls short of goals
5. I will reconstruct my life to be the best role model that I can be

STEP 2- PLOT an expressed plan of action that is designed to ensure a well rounded host of experiences.

STEP 3- PRACTICE self discipline as well as assert discipline through structure with consistent consequences within your child's life.

STEP 4- REEVALUATE the plan periodically in order to improve and make changes that best fit the environment and your child's strengths and weaknesses.

CURIOSITY: The 15th basic emotion

In addition to the 14 emotions covered in chapter 2, there is another emotion that is very essential to families and communities that shall be focused on separately. Curiosity is a natural emotion that all humans have. As a child develops, this curiosity serves as the **"seed of knowledge"**. Curiosity is a feeling of needing to know or understand the unknown. The explorative nature of an infant caters to the sponge like effect of their brains. As curiosity is satisfied with learning, the brain releases a good feeling chemical that rewards the person for their efforts. This chemical increases memory and plasticity in the hippocampus section of the brain.

Unfortunately different cultural experiences have a general tendency to enhance or stifle this seed of knowledge. Thus some cultures create a curious people who explore the world around them, and some cultural experiences create fear (feel-bad emotion) of the unknown. As you may be able to deduct, the cultures with the most curiosity will advance. The full understanding of this principle can be utilized to control the progress of an enemy. The next workbook produced by Black Family United in 2012 *(www.blackfamilyunited.org)* will focus on this point of the need for curiosity. But for now, make sure you are not stifling your individual or children's natural level of curiosity.

When your child has no interest in learning in school, and has no true interest to learn about any particular subject, topic or hobby, you may have a problem on your hands.

There are three types of thoughts that can occupy the mind:

Pacifying thought — Learning and participating in games that have specific rules of engagement. The successful interaction does not involve creativity, yet it involves practice to perfection of a set feat. For example: video games or basketball.

Destructive thought — Thoughts that create actions or feelings that do not benefit anyone in the long run. For example: Being abusive towards others or always expecting the worst outcome within situation, which often times becomes self fulfilling prophecies.

Constructive thought — Born from the seed of curiosity, this thought will ultimately create positive results. For example: If your child is curious about a particular subject, and you constantly encourage and reward that curiosity with learning opportunities, your child will gain a sense of expertise that will build the required self esteem which can transfer to any aspect of life in the future.

FAMILY TABLE OF CONTENT: A Suggestion, An Example:

Create a table of contents page to be the first page of your family diary. List all the things you want to expose your family to. This plan can be implemented by anyone without conflict in subject matter due to the fact that the parents create the categories. Hence, each family creates this table of contents according to their values and beliefs. To start, parents should discuss with trusted relatives and friends for their input on creating a list. The parents should take a sheet of paper and brainstorm on what important topics and experiences they should expose their children to.

Once you have a table of contents, make it the first page in a three ring binder. Give each of your children their own three ring binders. The parents use the list as a reminder, and periodically ask the children to write about a recent experience that the family has shared. The age that you start your children with their own binder should depend on their maturity to take this project seriously. I suggest 7 to 9 years old. For the younger children, you may want to allow them to draw a picture of what they remember.

As the family has similar experiences at different times of their youth, their writing will be placed in the binder according to the order on the table of content. With experiences of the same category, have the children place the most recent experience behind the older ones. They may witness their progressive advancement as they review older works. You may have to assist the children in organizing the binder according to the order stated on the table of contents that you created. This will teach them organizational skills and eventually they will be able to keep the order themselves.

These binders will turn into a way to cultivate ideas, thoughts and discussions. I'd suggest you make a rule to never read your children's folders, except when they agree to share an entry with the family for discussion. This will eliminate the pressure to write what you want to hear. The hopes are that if done sparingly enough (5 to 10 times per year), they will take pride in their writing and maybe even write in it without your suggestion. I'd also suggest that you not make this a scheduled writing assignment. You may allow months to go by until the right experience occurs with a strong lesson to be learned. You can suggest that they use particular words in their writing. This will ensure that they are on the right path of capturing the information, as well as become an opportunity to extend their vocabulary.

When they become parents they can do the same with their children and have their own childhood binder to discuss with their children what they wrote when they were a child. This promotes relating better between the generations, and also encourages your impact on your grandchildren. *See my Table of Content below:*

Harris Balanced Family Life Plan
For Clarity, Focus & Confidence in every aspect of life

I Personal
   Health
   Happiness
   Wellbeing
   Leadership

II Family virtues
   Traditions
   Holidays/Birthdays
   Family Time
   Family Meals
   Events
   Family Emotional Support
   Encouragement — belief in each other
   Mutual respect — listen for understanding

III Friends and socializing
   Who are your friends and why
   Who is no longer your friend and why
   What kind of friend am I
   Peer pressure
   Boy-Girl relationships

III Intellectual pursuit
   Traditional Education
   Family wisdom, passing of learned experiences

IV Spiritual Growth
   Who is God
   Different religions
   What I think

V Financial
   Banking accounts
   Assets over Liabilities — Balance sheet w. Equity
   Managing wants vs. needs
   Asset accumulation, Credit score & Net worth

VI Civic Assets
   The roll of Government, and how to effectively participate
   Understanding and respecting personal fortune
   Giving to those less fortunate in an effective way
   Understanding how economics impact sub-cultures
   Understanding how sub-cultures impact economics

GOD GIVEN TALENT

Talent is a natural endowment or ability of a superior quality that one is born with (a gift from God). Parents can not create talent in their children. A parent's primary job in their child's life is to provide the bare necessities

> In my family, every time someone has a baby, each adult has an obligation to put $200 into our family college trust fund. This money can only be used for college tuition, but the fact that everyone buys into the value of college creates an expectation of college for every child in the family.

of survival. Once basic needs are secured, parents have the obligation to assist their children in discovering the talents that their child may possess. Once a talent is discovered, the parent should work with the child to enhance the child's talents with skill. Skill is a learned capacity that enhances ability. The interaction surrounding talents and skills are "opportunities to parent."

OPPORTUNITIES TO PARENT

Many disengaged parents are overwhelmed or consumed with attempting to provide the bare necessities to their children, or they have simply de-prioritized parenting. In either case, they fail to take or create the opportunities to parent. These moments are discoveries of talents that go uncultivated, or cut-short conversations that could have lead to a child's understanding of the world, or a missed opportunity for the parent to praise the efforts of the child that could create motivation and drive within the child. At these moments the struggles of the parent are passed to the child as the child suffers the consequence of the sins and shortcomings of the parent.

VICIOUS CYCLES OF NEGATIVE TRADITION

"I buy a particular brand of peanut butter because my grandmother used to buy it." Traditions bring comfort due to familiarity. Yet African Americans were first slaves that created new traditions out of necessity to survive that institution. Not all traditions passed from generation to generation are wise and most advantageous. For example, prior to 1865 and the emancipation of slaves, most slaves only had a first name. Once freed, many chose or were given the last name of their slave master. The slave master was the (father) ruler of the slave house. Slave master never discussed life with the slaves, never educated the slaves and they often beat the slaves into submission when they did not follow the rules of the slave master. Some parents to this day, raise their children in the same fashion. Punishing children without adequately discussing why is training (animals) as opposed to educating (humans).

78

CREATING TRADITION

Leaders of families have the power and obligation to diminish harmful traditions as well as create new traditions that enhance the family experience. As a single parent or a team of spouses, grandparent and extended family, a series of decisions shall be discussed and enacted with the purpose of creating positive loving learning experiences of interdependence and cooperation. You owe it to yourself; you owe it to your community; you owe it to your great grand children.

> My family celebrates Kwanzaa every year. Each time I learn something about a family member that I never know. I even learn more about me and how I feel about the importance of family and what that really means.

> On the first Sunday of each month, my adult children and I meet for Sunday dinner and we each read and discuss a verse in the bible.

> My family holds a "Rites of passage" ceremony for each 16 year old child. On the 16th birthday of each boy, the men in the family take the boy on a camping retreat. On the 16th birthday of each girl, the women of the family rent a hotel for the weekend.

Deliberate Parenting is asking yourself: What will I teach my children, that they will teach to their children?

CHAPTER NOTES

Thoughts, questions and solutions:

_____

_____

_____

_____

_____

Personal challenges covered in the chapter:

_____

_____

_____

Potential ways to create change in my life/house/community:

_____

_____

_____

_____

_____

_____

Action plan and accountability follow up dates:

_____   _____

_____   _____

_____   _____

_____   _____

_____   _____

_____   _____

_____   _____

_____   _____

_____   _____

Community

"An individual has not started living until he can rise above the narrow confines of his individualistic concerns to the broader concerns of all humanity."

Dr. Martin Luther King

"All kids need is a little help, a little hope and somebody who believes in them"

Magic Johnson

Community Defined: A Latin word that means "the gift of being together." This word has been defined in over 90 ways since its origin. For the purpose of this book we shall take its original meaning and use that as a starting point as well as a goal to reacquaint ourselves.

Community	A group of people who often times share commonalities such as: kinship and a common genealogical blood line
Culture	Common appreciation of art, music, expression, foods, customs, clothing, religious beliefs, as well as common emotional responses
Location	Living within a geographic proximity
Social cohesion	A bond between one another that incites pleasurable interaction
Common Identity	Being associated with one another by outsiders. Reaping common benefits and suffering disadvantages by outsiders together.
Economic interdependence	Working together for the sustainability of all members

Within this broad definition of community, we can begin to see where the African American community is falling short of its communion. The most impactful deficiency is the lack of economic interdependence. As a community, African Americans have internalized the racism that used to exist towards them, as they began to discriminate against themselves. As racism and segregation was diminished, African Americans began to spend and invest their money outside of their own community. Their struggles of inclusion won them entrance into the mainstream markets. They left their communities to shop and purchase goods and services from other communities; therefore intensifying mistrust and spite for one another through the years.

Economic interdependence is the ability of a group to trust one another and work together effectively to provide goods and services in exchange for monetary gains that are further maintained within the community. As people of a certain community spend money in other communities, there is a leakage of money outward. The money spent in a different community went to paying the wages of others. These monies were spent to pay other peoples rents, tuitions and investments. The lack of prosperity within a particular community increases the difficulties to employ people in that community so that the funds created are maintained and spent multiple times for the benefit of the community.

PLAYING YOUR ROLE

What is required is a pool of people with various skill sets. For example: 5% of the population must be intelligent innovators who can create opportunities through their vision. 20% of the population must be respectable with strong communication skills. These people need to acquire specific organizational skills, such as accounting, marketing, and business management. 20% of the population must have intellectual trade knowledge, such as science, biology and engineering. Another 20% must have technical trade skills that are common to post-high school trade school. A large portion of the remainder must have the ability and focus to work a hard and honest day's work consistently. The smaller the percentage of "dead weight" people in a community, the better the community will become, due to the less likelihood of crime and additional expense to guard against or provide for the basic needs of the dead weights.

DEAD WEIGHT

Those people within a community who, due to low self esteem, low academic preparedness or general disenfranchisement, become a nuisance to the community. Each person should take on the responsibility to provide not only for their own basic needs, but to provide for the needs of those who they build a family structure with. As a community becomes weighted down while dealing with the addictions and bad-feeling emotions of these people, it loses focus and opportunity to improve economically, socially and morally.

This dead weight is what makes the people of the community prefer to leave the community to spend money, work and live. This exodus of the stronger people, leaves behind a growing ghetto of inopportunity and despair.

HOW TO REVERSE THIS TREND

First we must look at the source of this dead weight. Of the people who comprise our communities, we know who fills our prisons, we know which neighbor is most likely to rob us, and we know who is on public assistance. As we evaluate their life's situation, we can discover patterns that contribute to such outcomes. In fact, in discussing the ills of society with this group, they themselves will often tell you the precise source of their issues. So if we know the "who", and we know the "how", why have we not found the "what now"? The answer lies in the exodus. The exodus states that the goal is not to fix the community, but to get out of the community. This is a great solution. In raising children and providing safety, comfort and an improved lifestyle, the aspirations of moving up are commendable.

RECYCLING THE BLACK DOLLAR

As the population of upwardly mobile African Americans leave the economically deprived communities that they were raised in, they either assimilate into a mixed community, or into a relatively economically advanced African American community. Again, this is a great solution. The question becomes, have they reduced the amount of animosity and reluctance to work together with other African Americans? Are the most successful among us, socially conscientious enough to work together in a harmonious way? Or even at the higher levels of African American society, is there a reluctance to cooperatively work together for the common good of a fractured African American community?

If we study other minority groups, most of them have managed to create an interdependence that creates opportunities and assistance within their group. African Americans integrated into the U.S. economy by asking and begging white America to accept them. Throughout the African American struggle, there has always been two extreme philosophies, the first is integration (Fredrick Douglass, WEB Debuis and Martin Luther King Jr.), and the second is separation (Marcus Garvey and Malcolm X) . Yet the most effective plan at this point in history would be a middle ground between the two. A focus on gaining access to capital and opportunity, with a consciousness to contribute to growth and participation by all levels of the group. If African Americans can not care enough to help their own, support their own, and raise their own, who else should?

Being between two different socioeconomic groups, or two different cultures, one may have a choice of what aspects of each group's tendencies or qualities they'd like to adapt or disregard. This chapter on Community should compel thought of what choices should be made within such transitions. Just as a group should never reject a cultural custom simply because of which culture created it, they should never accept one simply because of which culture created it. Every culture has its good and bad qualities. The culture which is the best, is the one that has cultural leaders that implement positive cooperative change. The most influential cultural leaders of the African American people of today are mostly comprised of young fatherless, moral-less or uneducated entertainers. This fact is the biggest threat to the African American people. The promoting of a destructive lifestyle will only lead to destruction.

African Americans should never give up hope for all levels of the African American community. The upwardly mobile citizens should take-on the responsibility of advancement of not only themselves, but the community as well. A large improvement would simply be to look at one's finances and predetermine and ensure that 15% or 20% of personal income will be spent patronizing African American businesses or contributing to the betterment of those less fortunate.

By patronizing African American professionals, restaurants, investment brokers, auto dealers and the like, African Americans are giving back to their own community. That consistent demand for products and services will bring stability to those Black businesses. Consumers can then hold Black businesses accountable to provide opportunities for advancement for other African Americans. Jewish various temples disseminate "chits" which are monetary units that are redeemable at Jewish businesses. This encourages recycled dollars and stabilizes business and jobs. African Americans have large church structures that may easily advent such a marketing institution.

Why haven't we?

CUSTOMER SERVICE AND WORK ETHIC

Some African Americans believe that service and professionalism is sacrificed when doing business with many Black owned businesses. As well, African American business owners find it difficult to maintain a qualified, committed and competitive African American staff. So the question becomes, which of the following groups must sacrifice and struggle until the African American community is sufficient:

> African American business- focusing on training an African American staff to be more effective and efficient to improve the quality of the work force, work ethic and entrepreneurial spirit.

> African American customers- dealing with substandard or overpriced goods and services until black businesses are able to be as efficient as their competitors

> The African American community- As African Americans choose not to support Black businesses, the African American community continues to lose its economic viability.

Some group(s) will have to suffer the immediate effects of change, yet the long run outlook may be altered for the better if a conscious and assertive effort is given by the entire community. This would be a true Black Economic Empowerment Movement. An element of this movement will be in my next workbook, "Entrepreneur." This workbook will focus on educating a young population to become masters of their universe in order to compete and win.

ECONOMIC EMPOWERMENT is defined by three elements that the African American community is deficient in:

Motivation | Education | Cooperation

Historically as slaves, Africans from many different countries and customs were housed in common slave quarters. They all had different languages and did not share a kinship. Yet as their struggles united they adapted for the sake of survival. Over the 250 years and 14 generations of enslavement, there was a bonding culture that unified the people of struggle.

Culture is heavily shaped by the peoples understanding of the world they live in. Within the slave period, education, marriage and independent commerce was forbidden. Thus, some of the customs practiced were not the best for long-term prosperity. And why would they be, when life's daily struggle was so overwhelming and having control over one's own future was nonexistent?

As freed people, African Americans had the opportunity to change their culture to benefit their long-term prosperity. So they pursued education with the opening of thousands of schools and Black colleges. They pursued land grants to accumulate wealth for their families; and they pursued legal protections under the law.

EDUCATION 1865-1965

Prior to the end of the Civil War, in most Southern states and some Northern states it was illegal, to the point of death, to educate slaves. However, the few slaves and free Black people that were

> *"Education is the passport to the future, for tomorrow belongs to those who prepare for it today"*
>
> **Malcolm X**

educated were educated by the determination of their own will and with the assistance of local citizens within their community. There were no public school systems for Blacks.

Despite having to risk their lives and wrestle with the social and economic challenges presented to them, after slavery ended, African Americans pursued education with great ferocity. They understood that education dissolved the mysteries of the world and suited them with the intellectual armor to challenge white supremacy. They pursued education with the opening of thousands of elementary schools and a few Black universities throughout the nation. This was the beginning of a tumultuous love affair with Blacks seeking education.

After the Civil War and during Reconstruction, public schools were built and Blacks were legally permitted to attend segregated schools. In spite of limited access to economic resources, ill-equipped segregated schools successfully educated Black students to develop self-reliance and academic excellence.

 In 1881, Booker T. Washington opened the Tuskegee Normal and Industrial Institute for black students. His main objective was to provide the students with practical skills as well as a solid academic education. To promote self-reliance, the school's core curriculum included such courses as brick making, agriculture, carpentry and plumbing, as well as the standard academics of the time. Booker T. wanted his students to acquire all the necessary life skills to make them valued citizens of their communities.

For the next seventy-three years, until Brown vs. the Board of Education in 1954, public schools remained segregated. However, due to the cultural commitment to education, African Americans persevered.

The public school system has not been kind to the African American population. After Brown vs. the Board of Education court decision, many public schools were closed down by local city governments; the all white schools were re-opened as private entities, just to keep from having to admit African American. The Black schools that were closed remained closed.

African American parents believed that desegregating the public school system would afford their children the best opportunity to receive a first class education. But as we observe many public schools today are just as segregated as they were in 1954. Additionally, the high school drop-out rate for African American males in inner cities as of 2010 was 50%. The success of the African

American community should not be dependant upon the total dismantling of racist systems. The success must come in spite of it.

Education starts in the home, and is reinforced in the schools. Without a positive, supporting environment in both the home and school, learning becomes increasingly difficult. This is why the community is an essential part to holding households, parents, schools and teachers accountable. Hence the community must have cohesive cooperation.

LAND OWNERSHIP- "FORTY ACRES AND A MULE"

Land ownership is a vital asset to all successful communities, whether it is for producing life sustenance or to be leveraged to produce other opportunities. Land ownership is one of the cornerstones of empowerment, self destiny and wealth creation.

In January 1865, prior to the end of the Civil War, General William T. Sherman responded to the pleas of freed slaves for land. He issued his famed Field Order Number 15, setting aside a huge section of abandoned land along the Georgia and South Carolina coast for African American families on forty acres plots. With the war coming to an end and having no further need for the army mules, he offered one army mule to each head of household of the newly created Black landowners.

Some African Americans obtained land, but many of them were forced to relinquish their forty acres to the original white owners once they returned from the war. However, some African Americans were able to maintain the property.

On March 3, 1865, to address the calamitous conditions of formerly enslaved Americans, Congress formed the Bureau of Refugees, Freedmen and Abandoned Lands, commonly known as the Freedmen's Bureau. This entity was led by Major General Oliver Howard (Howard University's name sake) to provide temporary assistance to former slaves. The bureau provided services such as medical care, food, schools, and legal services. However, land management was the Bureaus central concern. Congress allowed the Freedmen's Bureau to sell only 5 to 10 acre tracts to freed slaves. As a result, tens of thousands of African Americans became land owners for the first time. Unfortunately, after the death of President Lincoln many of these new land owners were forced to give back their lands to the former slaveholders, by the new incoming administration.

The peak years for land ownership by African Americans, was 1910 to 1915. Collectively, African Americans owned 15 million acres of land of which 218,000 African American farmers were full or part owners. A steady decline of land ownership began for African Americans after 1915 as they began the first wave of the Great Migration North. By 1992, the US Census of Agriculture reported there were 18,000 black farmers left owning 2.3 million acres. Approximately an 85% reduction in land owned by blacks had accrued in seventy plus years.

As African Americans began to sell or abandon their farmland in the south to head north, they began the process of attempting to become home owners in the north. This proved to be difficult due to bank discrimination and the lack of supply of houses available to African Americans. The cities that African Americans populated were centered around the major train stations and industrialized business districts. Given this overpopulation, coupled with the plight of poverty intensified by the Great depression of the 1930's, the Federal Government began to mandate public housing projects in 1935.

Without enough jobs to sustain a community of workers, it was advantageous to build housing that could serve as an economic segregation line, between areas with declining home values and suburban areas that were focused on increasing property values. Suburban areas in the U.S. were a growing popularity during the late 1800's due to the advent of commuter electric railways. Yet demand increased even more once various cultures began to flood the inner cities.

WHITE FLIGHT

Given the fact that a large percentage of whites did not want to live around different ethnic groups, they would move from areas that had a potential for "infiltration." They did this to preserve their culture and their real estate investment values. If an area was thought to not attract minorities, this would essentially indicate that approximately 70% of the U.S. population would be potential buyers of the real estate in that area. Those 70% would bid the pricing up and keep the property and equity values high. Yet if it was perceived that a minority group wanted to infiltrate an area, than not only is culture and customs at risk, but there would be only 10% to 40%

of the U.S. population that would potentially buy in that area. This lack of demand reduced the need to bid prices upwards, and property values would fall.

This white flight worked to the advantage of African Americans, with the exception of those African Americans who were fleeing the Black culture and were trying to assimilate into the white culture. Those African Americans were usually the first to move into a white community. So in essence there were whites running from Blacks, and Blacks chasing the whites, and the majority of Blacks who were simply moving to a better Black neighborhood. The latter group was the ones who benefited the most. African Americans historically have been paid only a fraction of there white counterparts in wages; hence the lower the wage, the less real estate they could afford. So as whites moved away from areas, the property values decreased, becoming more aligned with the substandard wages earned by African Americans.

Since the 1940's, all the way until the real estate market collapse of 2008, African Americans have owned their own homes at a varying rate of 40% to 46% of the African American population, this in comparison to a 68% to 76% range for white Americans. As home ownership is vital to the economics of a family and a community, we should also consider additional factors regarding home ownership that makes a very big difference in how wealth is built:

AGE: *The average age of first time homeowners. If one groups average age is 26 and another is 39*

EQUITY: *The average percentage of equity held in real estate. A 60% equity holding is a substantial difference to 15%.(Equity- the value of the house minus what is owed to the bank)*

WILLED: *The average rate of homes being successfully passed to and maintained by offspring of original buyers.*

EXPENSE: *The average percentage of income the mortgage uses. If 50% of a family's income goes to the mortgage as opposed to 30%, they are in a more fragile financial situation.*

In studying the above rates, and implementing educational tools to improve these numbers, African Americans may accelerate their rate of economic progress going foreword.

LEGAL PROTECTIONS UNDER THE LAW 1865 – 1965

A slave had no, nada, zilch, nil, zero legal protection other than that extended to him by his owner. During Reconstruction (1865-77) the "Black Codes" were laws put in place mostly by Southern states after the Civil War to limit the human and civil liberties of Blacks. These laws were slowly dismantled but simultaneously replaced by Jim Crow. Congress passed laws at the national level for the states to adhere to and enforce regarding, African American citizens human and civil rights. These laws were intended to be observed by both government and private institutions:

1865:   Thirteenth Amendment abolished slavery

1866:   Civil Rights Act declared that people born in the United States are entitled to be citizens, without regard to race, color, or previous condition of slavery. It also stated that any citizen has the same right as a white citizen to make and enforce contracts, sue and be sued, give evidence in court, and inherit, purchase, lease, sell, hold, and convey real and personal property.

1868:   Fourteenth Amendment defined national citizenship and forbid the states to restrict the basic rights of citizens (gave citizenship to black people).

1870:   Fifteenth Amendment prohibits each state in the United States from denying a citizen the right to vote based on that citizen's "race, color, or previous condition of servitude."

1957:   Civil Rights Act, primarily a Voting Rights bill was to ensure that all African Americans could exercise their right to vote.

1964:   Civil Rights Act outlawed many forms of discrimination against blacks and women, including racial segregation. It ended unequal application of voter registration requirements and racial segregation in schools, at the workplace and by facilities that served the general public such as theaters, restaurants, and hotels.

1965:   Voting Rights Act; a landmark piece of national legislation that outlawed discriminatory voting practices that had been responsible for the widespread disenfranchisement of African Americans, mainly in the Southern states.

How many pieces of redundant legislation does one group of people need to have ratified in order for them to be recognized as citizen and afforded equal legal protection under the law? It is of utmost importance that all black males recognize that the American judicial system is not absolute and certain. Two identical cases can and often times do, render far different results when it comes to verdicts and sentencing. Variables such as socioeconomics, race, location where the crime was committed, who was the victim will often be determinate factors in the results.

It has also been successfully debated that the race a person is born into has a substantial influence on the amount of discrimination they experience in their lifetime. In a sociological experiment conducted by Steven Raphael; a black male with no criminal record applying for a certain job had a 14% chance of getting a callback for an interview, while a white male applying for the same job had a 34% chance of getting a callback for an interview. That indicates white men have more than double the chances than Black males with no criminal record. If both the black male and white male had criminal records of the same nature, the callback percentage was 5% and 17% respectively. This indicates an even larger discrepancy between ex-convicts with white males receiving more than triple the callbacks than Blacks.

There may be a perception among jury pools and court officials (which include African Americans) that believe that the African American culture/community lacks the cooperation necessary to increase potential rehabilitation of an ex-convict and reduce recidivism (repeat offenses). If the community that a person returns to from prison is capable of giving opportunities and discouraging criminal activity, there may be a reduction in sentencing and thus, the community plays a vital role in it's creation of the slave mentality explained below. This places the blame not only on the justice system or the criminal's personal choice, but also the community as well. History is against African Americans regarding the justice system; however, the answer to these problems will only come from the African American community through effective cooperation.

THE SLAVE MENTALITY

In today's society, there is a way to volunteer your services to a "slavery lifestyle." This option usually starts with a "slave mentality." The first choice is when a child is not given or does not take advantage of educational opportunities. The second choice is usually one's choice of friends. The last decision to volunteer for modern day slavery is to choose a life of crime. Once a person has a felony on his/her record, they not only have to do the time in prison, but they must live with the limits this title of ex-convict holds.

Given the lack of control over their future, slaves lost the need to plan for the distant future. They were more concerned with the immediate danger, oppression and struggle. Thus the mentality of a slave is simply the failure to plan your future, which prohibits substantial growth and perpetuates immediate struggles.

After slavery, opportunities to be formally educated grew slowly thanks to a few whites and educated blacks who founded schools for African Americans. In 1954, Thurgood Marshall fought a Supreme Court battle that stated separate was not equal. During the 1970's, after our legislative victories in the 1960's which were led by civil rights leaders such as Martin Luther King Jr., there was an extensive busing program that was met with opposition amongst the white population.

African Americans have always wanted and sought education. Each generation since slavery has encouraged, fought and died for the right of their children to be more educated than they were. This was a strong trend until the 1980's. The collapse of such a strong desire of parents to have their children educated was arguably caused by the chain of events of the following occurrences:

THE CHAIN OF EVENTS THAT BROKE THE LINK IN THE BLACK COMMUNITY

The civil rights movement of the mid 1960's that gave African Americans a sense of accomplishment and less of a need to support their own community.

The Great society created by President Lyndon Johnson in 1968 encouraged government dependency for families with children and no men in the home.

The Black power movement in the late 1960's created many militant factions of various political and social divides. Some of these organizations took on a criminal element for economic viability. They quickly changed from a positive movement of civil change for Black people, into bloods and crip gangs whose sole purpose was to obtain ill gotten gains.

The sex and drug culture of the 1970's which introduced the "I" society where personal gratification was more important than family or long term moral sacrifice.

The crack drug epidemic of the 1980's was the most powerful factor that altered the structure and function of the Black family.

During the 1970's, the racial income gap began to close. When Ronald Reagan took the U.S. Presidential office in 1980, manufacturing jobs began to disappear. The 1980's proved to be enriching for the upper middle class and depressing for the lower middle class. The income disparity began to rise again. Most African American families found at least one family member addicted to crack cocaine. Between people who partied to enjoy the good life, and those who partied to escape their struggle, there were many people who used drugs as a recreational escape. So crack was born out of the demand for an inexpensive and effective mind alteration. This epidemic left many children, motherless or fatherless. The drug trade placed many people on the track to prison institutionalization.

During the 1980's, twenty-eight U.S. States reported crack cocaine enforcement problems. Crack is so highly addictive that most people would get addicted from the very first use and would be unable to maintain a normal functional lifestyle. Thus, any children of the crack addicted person would not be able to depend on that parent for the much needed moral or financial support. Grandparents, aunts and uncles were required to step in and take on a larger role in raising children without a maternal instinct. Without this maternal instinct, abuse and molestation were increasingly probable.

From 1985 to 1994, the war on drugs created a drastic spike in the incarceration rate in the Black community. The drug of choice in the Black community was crack cocaine, which offenses where punished more severely than that of the predominantly white communities powder cocaine. The disproportionate amount of Black males flowing in and out of prison and having close contact with under-supervised young people, could have contributed to the sharp increase in teen pregnancy and molestation which may have encouraged homosexuality.

"CRACK BABY" was a term coined in urban hospitals to describe babies that suffered Prenatal Cocaine Exposure (PCE). Scientific studies are conflicting regarding the impact on the development of a child with PCE, yet it doesn't take a scientific study to inform an African American of the effects on his family that the crack epidemic has had. PCE has caused premature birth, birth defects and attention deficit disorder. Additionally, there are social implications of feelings of abandonment, neglect and the stigma of foster care which create behavioral problems for afflicted children.

Many children of that era may not have been biologically affected by PCE, yet the social environment may have been altered as teacher's focus and morale suffered due to the extra attention demanded by children with attention deficit disorder. PCE children often have social developmental issues that create a hostile environment for all children which could serve as an academic distraction.

94

The teenage pregnancy rate throughout the 1980's increased steadily. One of the direct contributors to this fact was the lack of parental supervision as families dealt with the fallout of crack cocaine. The teenage pregnancy rate reached its highest point in 1991, and began to fall thereafter. In 1991, the teenage pregnancy rate for African American girls was double that of the national average. Since then the teenage pregnancy rate has steadily fallen to 50% of the percentage in 1991. Yet there is an additional long term impact when parents are not financially or emotionally mature enough to start a functional nuclear family.

By 1990, the marriage rate in the black community was half of that in 1960. The divorce rate had doubled. The number of children living with extended family increased dramatically. The parents of that era were the beginning of a culture that did not emphasis progress to the next generation. The focus on education and strong moral values was lacking more than ever.

THE PARTY LIFESTYLE

As groups choose a high risk thrill seeking lifestyle such as promiscuity or mind altering substance use in order to escape, cope or enjoy life, they may be unknowingly volunteering for the next epidemic of addiction or disease that may occur. Thus, if African Americans as a group still embrace the "party lifestyle", they not only have failed to realize the impact crack and HIV has had on their cultural progress, but they are susceptible to similar occurrence in the future.

*"Our future as a people has never been in our control as much as it is
today. But the question remains, what will we do with that opportunity?"*

During the 1980's, the different African American generations turned against each other. The youth lost respect for the parents that abandoned them, and the uncles that abused them. Bullies and predators preyed on the defenseless, the older and wiser generation was not respected because they had no power to finance change. Relative to all African American generations prior, the African American community of the 1980's lacked motivation. Motivation is an emotion that pushes people to become something greater than they are currently.

There are people within the African American community that are motivated, and they do accomplish great things, yet they have to then decide if and how their success will benefit the

African American community. Often times, there is a lack of giving back. Being obligated to give to the community that you are from is a personal choice. Yet, within the African American community, without those shining examples, they are left with the deficiency of athletes and entertainers as role models for the youth.

Role models are not a requirement for motivation, but it helps. With having someone to respect and strive to be like, we are given a visual of this goal. This vision is what is required to have desire. Motivation is an emotion that is a combination of at least 3 of the 7 feel-good emotions. If the African American culture focuses on Ma'at and reduces reliance on bad-feeling emotions, motivation will be followed by success. It is not easy, it is not quick, but this success is guaranteed.

SOCIAL MEDIA

The internet has given birth to the information age. Technology is becoming second nature to younger generations as information and networking is at the fingertips of all society. This new wave has interrupted many business models and forced media outlets to rethink the way they do business. Music, movies and modeling is as easy as a camera phone and editing software. Anyone and everyone can produce media and place it on the internet for the world to see. People's lifestyle can be fully exposed on social media sites. The negative implications of this overexposure are often times miscalculated. Society should be conscious of the risk to future career opportunities and family [physical and spiritual] safety. The internet acts as a window into peoples personal lives, with no control as to who looks in. We must learn to harness, yet respect the power of social networking regarding business marketing and personal exposure.

This immediate access to potential markets should be a blessing to a people who have been locked out of so many opportunities by either the powers that be, or the negative power from within. We must see every evolution as an opportunity to not only benefit from financially, but an opportunity to enrich our souls and spirits. We have been taken advantage of and counted out for so long, now is the time in the history of America to unite under the banner of the Black National Anthem.

IN CONCLUSION

The challenges African Americans face in today's society have been created by non-Blacks, yet they are currently perpetuated by African Americans themselves. We have internalized the hate that resonates in how we respond emotionally to life's occurrences. African Americans have allowed the problems of one generation to be carried over and magnified into the next generation. Just as fads and trends go out of style, young African Americans must treat our bad habits as if they are out of style. They must be made aware of the shortcomings of their former generations. With such knowledge, they must equip themselves to love harder, live better and care more. If they don't do it, it won't be done, and the meek shall not inherit the Earth, but rather they will continue to be ruled by it in a perpetual state of being *a slave with a wage.*

I hope that I have structured and presented this guidebook in a fashion that will penetrate your thought patterns, encourage transformative understanding and result in enhanced ways of living. Most would agree that the needed changes in the Black community are almost impossible to resolve. Yet what is really unbelievable is the simplicity of the answer. It only takes a very small change in each one of us.

An *"Oh I get it now"* change

Live the change. For it is not the height of the mountain that should perplex you, it is the first step that should propel you.

Hold yourself to a higher standard | Embrace education

Innovate financial independence ventures

Support Black business | Practice sexual discretion

Resolve to relationship commitment | Challenge and engage the next generation

God's speed

CHAPTER NOTES

Thoughts, questions and solutions:

_____

_____

_____

_____

_____

Personal challenges covered in the chapter:

_____

_____

_____

Potential ways to create change in my life/house/community:

_____

_____

_____

_____

_____

Action plan and accountability follow up dates:

_____ _____

_____ _____

_____ _____

_____ _____

_____ _____

_____ _____

_____ _____

_____ _____

ACTIVITIES
To review the full list of activities, source materials and videos of activities go to:
www.Africanamericanidentity.org. Click on the ACTIVITIES button

Activity: You are a Skyscraper

Age range: 13 & up
Participants: All

Materials required:
Suggested - building materials to show strengths and visual aid.
Suggested – Class to review a Youtube video of a skyscraper being constructed time lapse

Preparation:
Ask the students if they know what an architect is. Discuss what an architect does and the importance of being a good architect when building a building. Ask the students if they know of, or been in a skyscraper. Talk about if the architect didn't do a good job in designing a skyscraper, many lives could be at risk. Tell the students to think about their house or apartment that they live in and how many floors is their building. Ask them if they wanted to build another one or two floors on top of their building, what would they need to do that. Instruct them that if they want to build upwards, they have to look at how strong the foundation of the structure is. The taller the building, the stronger the foundation has to be. Discuss what a foundation of a building is.

Activity:
A skyscraper is a tall building that reaches high into the sky and has multiple stories. "The skyscraper theory" states that each human being is like a skyscraper under construction. Try to envision if you where a skyscraper, what would you look like? How many floors would you have? What would you be made out of? Would you have an all glass exterior? Let's discover what your options are when building your "self" as a skyscraper. Below are the parts needed to start building your skyscraper.

The first part of a skyscraper is the most important part, the foundation. The foundation is the part of the skyscraper this is buried deep underground out of plain sight of the public. This foundation must be firmly attached to bedrock. Bedrock is the inner part of the earth that is below sand and dirt. By being grounded within bedrock, your foundation is strong and sturdy. The underground foundation of a person is the soul. The soul should be firmly grounded. Examples of the underground foundation or the soul are:

- Life force
- The difference between a live body and a dead body
- Energy that is contained in the body
- A connection with God/Higher power
- A rechargeable human battery that keeps the heart beating, the lungs breathing and the entire body functioning

The next part of a skyscraper is the support columns that are attached to the underground foundation "soul", but rise above the ground towards the sky. The support columns of a person are the persons "real self." Examples of support columns or real self are:

- Natural personality before people interject
- God given talents
- Capacity
- Ability
- Human Nature

So far, your skyscraper has all the elements that you were born with. This is who you are before anyone else changes who you are by telling you what to do, think and feel. From this point on, everything else added to your skyscraper is built with the assistance of other people, such as your family, friends, teachers and enemies.

The next step in building your skyscraper is to add the framing. The framing attaches to your support columns and give more stability to your structure. The inner walls and the exterior walls and windows are all attached to the framing. Unlike your foundation and support columns, you have a little more control over how this part is built. Examples of a skyscraper frame:
- Personality with environmental interjections
- Influence of family, friends and enemies
- False self
- Illusions

The next part that should be built is the floors. The floors are attached to the support columns as well as the framing. Each relationship you have is represented or built by that friend or family member.

Give examples of the floors

> Each relationship is a floor, who you associate with will determine how tall your building is, but the integrity of the people you associate with will determine how strong your structure is.

Give examples of the Windows

> Windows allow people on the inside to see well because of the sunlight. Windows will also allow people to see inside of you and see who you really are. They may see what type of person you are by talking to you or looking into your window; or they may see what you have and steal everything because you let the wrong people see what you have inside. So windows represent how much we expose of ourselves. Not to tell all of our business to everyone who is around, but to open up enough where you are not too dark and closed off to get depressed inside.

Give examples of the Walls

> Walls make rooms. If you have many walls, you may have many different rooms or compartments to your life, where many friends or activities are different. Another option is to have very few walls and there is a lot of open space, like a loft. This is when you may not have many different sets of friends or hobbies, but everyone knows and plays with everyone else in your life/building.

Building Materials (Strong, average, weak)
Philosophy of life is a decision to build your skyscraper out of flimsy temporary materials, or strong, sturdy and long lasting materials. Sample materials to building a self skyscraper are:

Love	Wisdom	Respect
Morals	Trust	Lies or deceit
Illusions	Ignorance	Materialism

Skyscraper Exercise:

- **Contractor Contractor-** The subject student is the owner of a plot of land and he wants to build a skyscraper, he already has his underground foundation laid. He also has the support columns erected. Now he needs to have others help him complete his structure. He is faced with many choices of who and how to construct his skyscraper.

  Give 3 students a flash card with the script written:
  - Contractor 1: I am a framing contractor and I want to bid for the job of building your skyscraper framing. I will build the frame out of clay for $1 million.
  - Contractor 2: I am a framing contractor and I want to bid for the job of building your skyscraper framing. I will build the frame out of wood for $2 million.
  - Contractor 3: I am a framing contractor and I want to bid for the job of building your skyscraper framing. I will build the frame out of steel for $3 Million.

  Have the class debate on which contractor the owner should use. Discuss how the following may be represented by each contractor: peer pressure, drugs, sex, not attending school, disrespecting self and others, love or lack of love, respect and honesty, long term thinking.

  Discuss the cost each contractor is charging for their services. This fee in a real relationship is usually friendship in return. Yet the higher the cost, the higher the returned commitment of friendship. So discuss building a reciprocating friendship and point out that they are building each others skyscraper simultaneously. Discuss the sameness of structures in a geographic area, tall buildings are usually together downtown, large houses are in the same neighborhood, small buildings are in the same neighborhood. Contractors are people who are close, and who are influential.

  "Birds of a feather flock together"

- **Friends Friends** - The subject student now has two new contractors come up to him and read from their flash cards:
  - I was your friend that built the 5th floor. I used very thin wood on the floor maybe because I really didn't like you, or maybe I really didn't like myself and didn't care about the quality of my work, or maybe I liked you at first but then you made me mad because I have a bad temper and when you make me mad, I'm going to get even and get you back. So I made the 5th out of very thin wood.
    - Instructor reads: So one month later, your floor caved in and your building was damaged. Now you have to rebuild, or just keep a big hole in your floor.

- I was your friend that built the 20th floor, I used very thick wood on the floor because I really like you. I think you are cool and I would never want your building to be damaged because of my work. I want the work that I do to be good work, and I want it to last forever. So I built the 20 floor to be strong, like our friendship. You can count on me and my work.

Have the class discuss the differences in the friendships and the long term effects of having both types of friends.

- **The roof** - The roof is the person that you are in a relationship with, like a husband/wife. This person's job is to protect you like a roof protects a building from bad things getting in. If a relationship ends, or divorce happens, it's like your roof has caved in and now everything inside can suffer damage.

- **Windows** – Discuss rumors and talking behind peoples backs and how that can hurt someone's feelings and damage them. A skyscraper can be built with a lot of windows, or very little windows. Windows represent how open a person is. How much light he/she lets into his/her life. Each person has an option to openly talk about what's going on with them, or to be secretive. Even the people inside the building can be left in the dark about how this person really feels about things. There is a balance between being private and being open to those people you can trust. Being able to express your feelings in a productive way is very important to building solid relationships and a solid skyscraper.

Activity: Win/Win Win/Lose

Age range: 13 & up
Participants: All

Materials required: N/A

Activity: Instructor to read off different scenarios below. The class is to determine which of the four below types of scenarios applies and discuss:

Scenario types: Win/Win   Win/Lose   Lose/Lose
                     Winner   Love/Hate   Loser

Scenarios:
- You have a lemonade stand on a hot summer day, the cost to you to make the lemonade is 5 cent. You sell each tall glass of lemonade for 50 cents each.

- You study 5 hours a day, each day so that you can do your best on your test. You do not go out with friends or watch television. Your hard work pays off and you receive an A on the test.

- Jack and Jill are boyfriend and girlfriend. They spend time together and hold hands. Jill makes Jacks favorite sandwich for Jack every day. Jack carries Jill's books home from school. They get along just fine and share everything. Then Jack breaks up with Jill. Now Jill is hurt and is angry with Jack. Due to the fact that Jack hurt her, she wants to get even with Jack. She pokes a hole in Jacks bicycle tire. Jack sees Jill flatten his tire, so he gets mad at her and starts to call her names. They both are mad and instead of focusing on calming down or not letting their hurt turn into hateful actions and hateful words, they decide to try to take their anger out on each other because they both want the other person to feel the hurt that the other person caused.

- Ken and James are both assistant managers at Pizza Hut. The manager position will be opening up in a few weeks, and they both want to be promoted to the higher position. Ken steals $50 out of James' cash register so that James comes up short $50 at the end of the day when they count the register money. This will make James look bad and increase Ken's chances of getting the promotion over James.

- Tina and Keisha both take biology and algebra together. Tina is good at biology, but struggles in algebra. Keisha is good at algebra, but struggles in biology. They both decide to tutor each other in the subjects they are strong in.

- Tim and Krystal are in a relationship together. After graduating high school, Krystal is accepted to a college in a different state. Tim doesn't want Krystal to leave. Krystal wants to go but have a long distance relationship. Tim breaks up with Krystal because he doesn't feel that the relationship will work.

- Chris and Trevon are best friends in high school. At a high school party one night, they are standing in a group with a bunch of friends. One of the boys in the group pulls out a bag of drugs. He takes some and passes it around. As Chris is handed the drugs he takes it and puts it up towards his face to take some. Before he can consume it, Trevon slaps Chris in the face, knocking the drugs out of Chris' hands, and shouts "what are you doing!" This upsets Chris and they begin to physically fight.

INTAKE - Student Status Report

Student Information

Student Name: _____ Student ID: _____

School/Group: _____ Instructor: _____
Report Start
Date: _____ Report
End Date: _____

Birthdate: _____ 3/6 month follow up date: _____

Follow up dates _____ _____ _____ _____ _____ _____ _____ _____

Background / Living situation / Special needs/interest:

_____
_____
_____
_____
_____
_____
_____
_____
_____

Developmental / Mental Status:

_____
_____
_____
_____
_____

Education / Academic Level:

_____
_____
_____
_____

Evaluators notes:

_____
_____
_____
_____
_____
_____
_____

Short-Term Action Items	Due Date	Status

Long-Term Goals	Due Date	Progress

Concerns

Accomplishments